# MEMORIES OF YANKEE STADIUM

Scott Pitoniak

TRIUMPH
BOOKS

No part of this publication may be reproduced, stored in a retrieval system, or transmitted in any form by any means, electronic, mechanical, photocopying, or otherwise, without the prior written permission of the publisher, Triumph Books, 542 South Dearborn Street, Suite 750, Chicago, Illinois 60605.

Triumph Books and colophon are registered trademarks of Random House, Inc.

Library of Congress Cataloging-in-Publication Data

Pitoniak, Scott.
  Memories of Yankee Stadium / Scott Pitoniak.
      p. cm.
  Includes bibliographical references.
  ISBN-13: 978-1-60078-056-1
  ISBN-10: 1-60078-056-3
  1. Yankee Stadium (New York, N.Y.)—History. 2. New York Yankees (Baseball team)—History. I. Title.
  GV416.N48P58 2008
  796.357068747'1—dc22

                                                              2008000377


This book is available in quantity at special discounts for your group or organization. For further information, contact:

**Triumph Books**
542 South Dearborn Street
Suite 750
Chicago, Illinois 60605
(312) 939-3330
Fax (312) 663-3557

Printed in U.S.A.

ISBN: 978-1-60078-056-1

Design by Sue Knopf

Front cover painting © Legendary Sports Prints, LLC
www.sportslithographs.com

All photos courtesy of Getty Images, except where otherwise indicated.

*To my father, Andrew Pitoniak.*

*Thanks, Dad, for taking me out to the ballgame.*

A native of Rome, New York, and a magna cum laude graduate of Syracuse University, **Scott Pitoniak** has received more than 100 journalism awards. He has been named one of the top columnists in the nation by the Associated Press Sports Editors and is the author of 10 books. Scott attended his first game at Yankee Stadium in 1966, and he has been making annual pilgrimages to The House That Ruth Built ever since. He is married to the former Beth Adams and has two children, Amy and Christopher.

# CONTENTS

# FOREWORD

When I attended my first World Series game at Yankee Stadium on October 8, 1956, I had no idea I would be witnessing one of the most memorable contests in baseball history. I was merely going there that crisp autumn day to root against the hated Yankees. See, as a 16-year-old from Brooklyn, I had grown up a fan of Willie Mays and the New York Giants, so my allegiances were grudgingly with the Dodgers because I was a National League guy. Plus, I knew it would be so sweet to celebrate with my fellow Brooklynites if the Dodgers could knock off the Yankees again, just as they had done in 1955 when "next year" finally arrived in the borough of my birth.

But when the game reached the top of the ninth inning and the Dodgers still hadn't gotten a hit off Don Larsen, I began silently rooting for baseball history to be made. Like the 65,000 other fans in the stadium that day, I knew there had never been a no-hitter in the World Series, and I thought it would be cool to be on hand for the first one. So, even though Larsen pitched for the team I couldn't stand, I have to admit that a part of me was happy he wound up throwing a perfect game on the day I was there.

It's funny how life works out. Forty years later I returned to Yankee Stadium as the manager of the team I grew up rooting against. And I sat in the home-team dugout pulling for David Wells and David Cone to put the finishing touches on perfectos, which they did. It was amazing when Don Larsen threw out the ceremonial first pitch to Yogi Berra before Cone's no-hitter, and after Wells's gem, we learned that Larsen and Wells had attended the same San Diego high school.

There have been many special moments for me during my career, both as a player and as a manager, but perhaps the most special of those moments occurred at 10:56 on the night of October 26, 1996. That's when, after more than 4,000 games as a player and a manager, I finally was able to experience what my older brother Frank had experienced 39 years earlier with the Milwaukee Braves—winning a World Series title. As I led my team on a victory lap around the stadium, I thought about what a long, emotional journey it had been.

We, of course, would go on to win three more World Series championships and make the playoffs all 12 years that I managed the Yankees. I feel privileged to have called Yankee Stadium my office during that stretch. It obviously is the most special and historic ballpark in America.

—Joe Torre

# ACKNOWLEDGMENTS

**A** book is a true team effort. And I was fortunate to have a heck of a team behind me during this journey back in time.

A doff of the cap to Bob Snodgrass, Laine Morreau, Tom Bast, and the other dedicated folks at Triumph Books for making this project a reality.

A hug for my loving wife, Beth Anne, whose support and meticulous copy editing helped me get through the difficult stages and maintain some semblance of sanity.

A handshake for Joe Torre, one of the classiest people I've dealt with in my 35 years as a sportswriter.

A pat on the back for artist Bill Purdom, whose cover illustration brought me back to days of yore.

And high fives to the scores of people who were kind enough to share their memories with me.

I'd especially like to thank the following folks for their help: Jim Abbott, Joe Altobelli, Marty Appel, Raymond Berry, Steve Bradley, Bob Costas, Harvey Frommer, Frank Gifford, Christopher Granozio, Chuck Hinkel, Joe Horrigan, Katie Leighton, Doug

Mandelaro, Jim Mandelaro, Danny Mantle, David Mantle, John Maroon, Dan Mason, Matt Michael, the New York Yankees, Keith Olbermann, Phil Pepe, Amy Pitoniak, Christopher Pitoniak, David Ramsey, John Ricco, Cal Ripken Jr., Ed Shaw, Curt Smith, Lilly Walters, and Bob Wolfe.

# INTRODUCTION

The No. 4 train emerged from the clammy subway tunnel and rumbled up the rusty, elevated tracks like an old-fashioned roller coaster. Before hissing to a halt high above River Avenue and 161st street in the South Bronx, I caught a glimpse of the mountainous, white concrete edifice.

"There it is! There it is!" I exclaimed with the wide-eyed wonderment of a young boy. "Yankee Stadium! The House That Ruth Built! The most famous ballpark in the world!"

My kids appeared mortified by my behavior.

"Dad, be quiet," my 11-year-old daughter, Amy, implored, poking me in the ribs. "You're embarrassing us."

"Yeah, Dad," chimed in my eight-year-old son, Christopher. "Settle down before you have a heart attack."

There was no danger of that, though the palpitations were similar to ones I felt 32 years earlier when my father and I made this same baseball pilgrimage for the first time.

"It's just a big building," Amy said, her logical assessment sounding sacrilegious to an aging baby boomer who grew up fully intending to replace Mickey Mantle in center field.

"Amy, you don't understand," I protested mildly as we walked off the train. "It's more than a building. Much more."

As we pushed through the turnstiles beyond the left-center-field fence two hours before the first pitch that July 4, 1998, I clutched my son's hand the way my dad had clutched mine so many summers ago. Faster than you could say, "How about that!" I had been taken back, back, back in time.

► ► ►

There are certain "firsts" you never forget. Your first kiss. Your first home run. Your first car. Your firstborn.

You definitely can count my maiden journey to the stadium among my indelible "firsts."

September 17, 1966—Bobby Richardson Day—was the first time I set foot in the big ballpark in the Bronx, and I remember it as vividly as if it happened 41 seconds rather than 41 summers ago. I had never seen a building so massive, so cavernous. You could have fit my entire hometown of Rome, New York (population 50,000), in there and still had room for thousands more.

The blueness of the seats and the greenness of the grass had a visceral impact on me. It was similar to what I felt when I witnessed that scene from *The Wizard of Oz* when the film, in a snap, magically switches from dull black-and-white to brilliant color.

My initial trip to the stadium featured a prodigious exhibition of power by the Mick himself during batting practice. I

*An aerial view of a packed Yankee Stadium in 1955. The House That Ruth Built became much more than just a baseball stadium; it became a historical epicenter during its more than 80 years of existence.*

watched in jaw-dropped amazement as the blond-haired, blue-eyed, biceps-bulging Mantle muscled BP offerings into the far reaches of the upper deck. I couldn't help but notice a different sound to the balls he hit. It was an explosion rather than a crack of the bat. White ash against horsehide never sounded so good.

All those memories came rushing back as I waited in line at Monument Park in the renovated stadium with my kids decades later. The Yankees were taking batting practice at the time, and Scott Brosius deposited a home run 10 feet from us. An usher named Tony picked up the ball, walked over to Amy, and said, "Honey, this one has your name on it." My incredulous daughter couldn't believe her good fortune. The radiance of her smile was exceeded only by the afternoon sun.

With time to kill before the first pitch, I took my son up the ramps to the third deck in right field. He started to run, and I shouted for him to slow down so he wouldn't fall. The instant the words left my lips, it occurred to me that my dad had once issued this very same warning near this very same spot. Yankees manager Joe Torre often said there are ghosts in this building. I realized he wasn't just talking about the ghosts of Ruth, Gehrig, and Joe D., but also the ghosts of loved ones who had moved on.

Christopher and I went halfway up the steep steps in the upper deck, and I pointed to the back row and told him about home runs Mickey used to launch up here. My son looked uneasily down at the field and toward home plate, more than 450 feet away. He was more concerned about returning to the comfort of a lower deck than listening to history lessons from his old man.

The game that day was closely contested, with the Yanks eking out a 4–3 win on a blown ninth-inning call against the Baltimore Orioles. My son was disappointed he didn't witness any home runs, but he was pleased to see Yankee shortstop Derek Jeter make an acrobatic play and drive in three runs with two base hits.

Midway through the game, I closed my eyes briefly and tried to imagine my dad seated next to me, and the ornate, faded, blue-green façade that used to hang from the stadium roof, and the Mick in the batter's box mashing baseballs into the clouds. I wished Andrew Pitoniak could have shared this moment with his son and grandchildren. I wished he could have sat there with us. I would have told him how much I appreciated all the times he made those eight-hour round-trips from Rome to the Bronx for Sunday afternoon doubleheaders. I would have told the mechanic with the eighth-grade education and the heart as big as this ballpark how much I loved him.

In August 1970 he and I visited this baseball cathedral together a final time. We saw the Yankees retire Casey Stengel's No. 37 jersey that day. Six months later, Dad's heart beat a final time. It would be more than a decade before I would muster the gumption to return to the big ballpark in the Bronx.

► ► ►

Sinatra's "New York, New York" blared over the loudspeakers as my kids and I streamed out of the stadium with thousands of others. I had purposely made sure that Amy and Christopher's first major league baseball game would be experienced at Yankee

Stadium. I was thankful they had indulged my nostalgic emotions, that their old man hadn't embarrassed them too badly.

Perhaps one day they'll realize that no ballpark in the world—not even the Roman Colosseum—can hold a Louisville Slugger to this place.

Perhaps one day they'll understand why this edifice was so important to their dad and tens of millions of others who worshipped baseball gods and other deities here.

The motivation for writing this book wasn't merely to take a trip down memory lane—though, I must admit that certainly has been a most enjoyable trek—but also to provide future generations with an appreciation for an architectural wonder that became as much a part of the Big Apple as the Statue of Liberty, the Empire State Building, and Carnegie Hall.

Sadly, the wrecker's ball will replace the fastball and the curveball and bring down The House That Ruth Built after the 2008 season. A new Yankee Stadium will step to the plate across the street.

And, while it is sure to be much more fan-friendly, player-friendly, and owner-friendly, it will never be able to equal the history and tradition of its predecessor.

See, the original Yankee Stadium was more than just a building. Much more. It was hallowed ground. A rare place that could take you back, back, back in time.

—*Scott Pitoniak*
*November 5, 2007*

# A BRIEF HISTORY
# OF YANKEE STADIUM

I t is known as "The House That Ruth Built," but it easily could be called "The House That John McGraw Forced the Yankees to Build."

After all, if it weren't for the pugnacious, vertically challenged New York Giants manager, the Yankees might have become the Manhattan Mashers rather than the Bronx Bombers. They might have written their unparalleled baseball history in the Polo Grounds rather than Yankee Stadium.

From 1913 to 1922, the Yankees rented the Polo Grounds in upper Manhattan from McGraw's Giants. And the shared arrangement was working just fine until Yankee owners Jacob Ruppert and Tillinghast L'Hommedieu Huston decided to make Boston Red Sox owner Harry Frazee a dramatic offer he couldn't refuse. Frazee, whose true passion was the theater, was in need of cash. So, in the fall of 1919, he approached Ruppert and Huston, seeking a loan of a half-million dollars, and the Yankee owners countered with an offer of $115,000 in cash and a personal loan of $350,000 in exchange for the Red Sox's star pitcher and slugger, Babe Ruth. A day after Christmas that year, the transaction was consummated.

Talk about the perfect storm. The time, the place, and the performer couldn't have been more perfectly aligned. The Roarin' '20s were about to unfold, New York had become America's most populous and prominent city, and Ruth was on the verge of changing baseball forever with his booming bat and larger-than-life personality.

During the summer of 1920, the Babe posted otherworldly statistics— 54 home runs, 137 runs batted in, and a .376 batting average. Although the Yankees finished in third place, the fans didn't care. Roughly 1.3 million of them flocked to the Polo Grounds to witness the Sultan of Swat slug homers farther and more frequently than anyone had before. The Yankees wound up drawing 350,000 more spectators than their landlords did.

This scenario repeated itself the following season as Ruth's popularity soared higher than one of his majestic, cloud-kissing home runs. The Yankees won their first American League pennant in 1921, but lost to McGraw's Giants five games to three in a best-of-nine World Series.

Although the Giants had maintained their title as baseball's best team, they had been supplanted as baseball's most popular

> **OFF THE WALL**
> *New York Evening Telegram* sportswriter Fred Lieb is the man credited with nicknaming Yankee Stadium "The House That Ruth Built."

team by Ruth's Yankees—a situation the seething McGraw found intolerable.

After being significantly outdrawn by the Yanks for a second consecutive season, the manager known in baseball circles as "Little Napoleon" decided he could take no more. He handed the Yankees their eviction notice, telling them that their lease would be up following the 1922 campaign.

"If we kick them out," McGraw reasoned, "they won't be able to find another location on Manhattan Island. They'll have to move to the Bronx or Long Island. The fans will forget about them, and they'll be through."

The eviction notice didn't cause the Yankee owners to panic. If anything, McGraw had done them a favor, providing them with the impetus they needed to build a spectacular new ballpark unlike any that had been constructed before. Ruppert sensed that the baseball industry was about to take off. He also knew that in Ruth he had the perfect drawing card to pack the new place. The timing couldn't have been more exquisite.

As McGraw had predicted, finding a location for the new ballpark presented problems. Initially, the Yankees considered a lot in Long Island City and the Hebrew Orphan Asylum in Upper Manhattan, but both deals fell through, as did the idea of constructing the stadium over the Pennsylvania Railroad Tracks in downtown Manhattan. (An idea which, by the way, was floated again when the Yankees, Mets, and football Jets went looking for new stadium sites at the turn of the 21st century.)

Ruppert and Huston finally settled on a nondescript lumber yard in the South Bronx, just across the Harlem River from the Polo Grounds. They purchased the 10-acre tract for $675,000 from the estate of William Waldorf Astor. Who knew that the lot, which had been a farm before the Revolutionary War, would become baseball's most fertile ground, producing an unequaled bumper crop of championships and Hall of Fame players and managers?

Ruppert's grandiose vision called for a ballpark that would be every bit as imposing as the iconic Roman Colosseum. The original plans drawn up by the Osborne Engineering Company of Cleveland, Ohio, called for a triple-decked structure that would be enclosed all the way around. The architects boasted they would design a stadium that would be visible only to the spectators inside the arena and aviators flying above it. But soaring costs and the closing off of the light from outside the park forced those plans to be scaled back. The new renderings called for the decks to extend only to each foul pole, meaning the open outfield area would be visible to passengers on the elevated subway trains and to residents of high-rises that were beginning to sprout just beyond River Avenue.

Despite the downsizing, the edifice still would be able to seat 70,000 spectators, making it roughly the same capacity as Rome's world-famous Colosseum. The most distinctive feature of the new ballpark would be the 16-foot decorative copper façade that would adorn the roof covering the third deck.

To take full advantage of Ruth's left-handed power, Ruppert instructed the architects to place the right-field foul pole just 295 feet from home plate. The power alley in right-center field also was made tantalizingly close, but dead center would be a ridiculous 490 feet away. Though the left-field foul pole was just 281 feet from home, the power alley in left bowed out quickly and was a near impossible distance of 460 feet in left-center. Right-handed batters would come to curse the unfairness of the park, calling the power alley "Death Valley," a place where even the most monstrous of drives would die in the webs of outfielders' gloves.

The stadium was built by the White Construction Company. The New York City–based firm received $2.5 million to erect the landmark, and the contract included the proviso that it must be completed by Opening Day 1923. Remarkably, the deadline was met. Work began on May 5, 1922, and was finished just 284 days later.

> **OFF THE WALL**
>
> The stadium hosted 30 world championship boxing matches. The first occurred on July 24, 1923, when lightweight Benny Leonard won by decision over Lew Tendler, while the last took place on September 28, 1976, when heavyweight Muhammad Ali defeated Ken Norton by decision. Heavyweight champion Joe Louis fought 11 matches there, more than any other boxer.

*April 18, 1923, marked the opening of Yankee Stadium. It was a bustling scene outside the stadium on this historic day.*

That was no small engineering feat, considering the volume of materials required to build the stadium. Nearly a million feet of Pacific Coast fir was transported through the Panama Canal to construct the outfield bleachers. More than 2,300 tons of structural steel and a million brass screws were needed to erect the first three-tiered arena in America, and the first ballpark to be called a stadium.

Yankee Stadium opened for business on April 18, 1923, and the Babe couldn't wait to christen his new baseball home. Before the game, he told reporters: "I'd give a year of my life if I can hit a home run in this first game in this new park."

In true Ruthian fashion, he smacked a three-run shot off Boston Red Sox right-hander Howard Ehmke in the bottom of the third inning. Much to Ruppert's delight, the ball sailed into the right-field bleachers—a place that would quickly become known as "Ruthville," and later "Gehrigville," after left-handed Yankees slugger Lou Gehrig.

According to the *New York Times'* account of the day, the stadium "trembled with noise as the big man circled the bases, soft-stepped across home plate, and lifted his blue cap at arm's length, the leading man on the biggest stage in the newest theater in town."

The Babe's blast, along with Bob Shawkey's three-hit pitching performance, catapulted the Yankees to a 4–1 victory and capped a festive day in which New York governor Alfred E. Smith threw out the ceremonial first pitch, and legendary conductor John Philip Sousa and the famed Seventh Regiment Band entertained the announced crowd of 74,217—the largest throng ever to witness a baseball game.

The following day, *New York Evening Telegram* sportswriter Fred Lieb called the stadium "The House That Ruth Built," and the name stuck.

Led by the Babe, the Yankees captured their third consecutive American League pennant and found themselves playing their former landlords, the Giants, in the World Series again.

On October 10, 1923, Yankee Stadium hosted its first of 37 Fall Classics, but the Series didn't start out the way the home fans had hoped. In this instance, Mighty Casey—Giants outfielder Casey Stengel—didn't strike out. Instead, he lashed a

*Babe Ruth demonstrates his classic swing at Yankee Stadium before a game in 1923.*

line-drive, inside-the-park homer that rolled past Bob Meusel and Whitey Witt in left-center. Though the ball had traveled nearly 450 feet from home plate, Stengel almost didn't make it around the bases in time. He nearly lost one of his spikes chugging home and had to slide in order to elude the catcher's tag.

Stengel, who would later become the Yankees' most successful manager, hit another game-winning homer before the Series ended and was slapped with a $50 fine by baseball commissioner Judge Kenesaw Mountain Landis after thumbing his nose at the Yankees dugout. Despite Casey's heroics, the Yankees—behind the Babe's three homers and eight walks— won the Series in six games. It would be the first of a mind-boggling 26 Fall Classics the Bronx Bombers would capture, prompting the stadium to also become known as "The Home of Champions."

> **OFF THE WALL**
> **Notre Dame played 24 football games at Yankee Stadium, posting a 15–6–3 record. Twenty-one of those contests were against Army, with the Fighting Irish going 14–4–3.**

The cantankerous McGraw clearly had struck out with his prophecy that the Yankees would shrivel up and disappear after vacating the Polo Grounds. Thanks to his paranoia and Ruppert's vision, the Bronx Bombers became America's most recognizable sports franchise, and their grandiose stadium is now as world-renowned as that ancient edifice in Rome.

The Yankees, with their unparalleled success and succession of Olivier-like actors such as Ruth, Gehrig, Joe DiMaggio, Mickey Mantle, and Derek Jeter, were the main tenants who made the ballpark as famous as Broadway.

**OFF THE WALL**
**Since its opening in 1923, 37 of 83 World Series have been played at Yankee Stadium. The Yankees clinched nine of their 26 Fall Classic titles at The House That Ruth Built.**

But many other performers and events also contributed to the stadium's unmatched aura and mystique.

This was the stage upon which legendary University of Notre Dame football coach Knute Rockne delivered his famous "Win One for the Gipper" halftime speech—which eight decades later remains the most inspirational and widely referenced motivational talk in sports history.

For 17 autumns, this was the gridiron home of the New York football Giants and the place where "the greatest game in history" was played—the 23–17 overtime victory by the Johnny Unitas–led Baltimore Colts over the "Gints."

This was the place where lords of the ring made a name for themselves. A total of 30 world boxing championships were decided at Yankee Stadium, with pugilistic icons such as Jack Dempsey, Joe Louis, Rocky Marciano, Sugar Ray Robinson, Carmen Basilio, and Muhammad Ali all duking it out at one time or another between the ropes on the makeshift canvas ring set up near second base. And none of those fights was more historically or socially significant than the one waged between Louis and German heavyweight Max Schmeling on June 22, 1938. As more than 80,000 spectators looked on, the Brown Bomber knocked out Schmeling in the first round, regaining his title and striking a blow against Adolf Hitler's theory of Aryan superiority.

The stadium also became a place where worshipping went beyond sporting gods, as two popes celebrated mass there, Billy Graham hosted religious crusades there, and 123,000 Jehovah's Witnesses convened there one day in the late 1950s, establishing a stadium attendance record that still stands.

When Big Apple officials sought a venue for a rally welcoming freedom fighter Nelson Mandela to the United States, they chose Yankee Stadium. When actor Kevin Costner looked for a ballpark to film his movie, *For Love of the Game,* he picked The House That Ruth Built. And when Oprah sponsored a healing vigil for devastated New Yorkers following the tragic events of 9/11, the big ballpark in the Bronx took center stage again.

U2, Pink Floyd, and Bronx-born Billy Joel all wound up rocking The House That Ruth Built in sold-out concerts, and opera stars Robert Merrill and Ronan Tynan made spectators misty-eyed with booming renditions of "The Star-Spangled Banner" and "God Bless America."

More than 200 million people have journeyed through the ballpark's turnstiles since it opened for business 85 years ago.

They, too, are a huge part of the building's legacy. They've witnessed some of the most extraordinary moments in the history of sports and New York City. And they have helped make Yankee Stadium into a Big Apple icon as recognizable as the Empire State Building, the Statue of Liberty, and Carnegie Hall.

It wound up becoming far grander than Ruppert had envisioned when he drew up plans following McGraw's eviction notice.

It wound up becoming the most famous sports arena in the world.

# 2

# MEMORABLE MOMENTS

**MAY 5, 1922**—The White Construction Company begins building the new $2.5 million Yankee Stadium with the edict that it must be completed in time for the ballclub's 1923 home opener. Remarkably, the New York–based builder completes the monumental task in just 284 days. It is the first three-tiered ballpark in American history and the first one to be called a stadium. For the first several years of its existence, it is known as "The Yankee Stadium."

**APRIL 18, 1923**—Legendary conductor John Philip Sousa and the famed Seventh Regiment Band entertain the crowd of 74,217 spectators, and New York governor Alfred E. Smith throws out the ceremonial first pitch. But it's Babe Ruth who steals the show. Displaying his trademark flair for the dramatic, the Babe christens the Yankees' cavernous new ballyard with a home run in the first game ever played there as New York beats Boston 4–1 behind Bob Shawkey's three-hit pitching performance. The following day in his game account for the *New York Evening Telegram*, sportswriter Fred Lieb describes Yankee Stadium as "The House

That Ruth Built," and the nickname continues to be used eight decades later.

**JULY 24, 1923**—A boxing ring is set up near second base, and Benny Leonard, one of the greatest lightweight boxers of all time, wins by decision over Lew Tendler as a crowd of 58,000 looks on in the first of 30 world title bouts at the stadium.

**OCTOBER 10, 1923**—New York Giants outfielder Casey Stengel hits an inside-the-park homer, giving his team a 5–4 victory over the Yankees in the first World Series game played at Yankee Stadium. Stengel's gapper rolls nearly 450 feet to the left-center-field wall, but despite the distance, Stengel barely makes it home safely, because as he chugs around third base, one of his spikes almost comes off.

**OCTOBER 15, 1923**—A year after being swept by the Giants (with one game ending in a tie), the Yankees redeem themselves by beating their crosstown rivals four games to two to capture their first of 26 World Series titles. The loss is especially hard for manager John McGraw to take because his team had dominated baseball for nearly a decade and had once served as landlords to the Yankees in the Polo Grounds.

**JUNE 1, 1925**—The lineup change drew scant attention from fans and reporters but would take on historical significance years later. Regular first baseman Wally Pipp was suffering from a headache, so Yankees manager Miller Huggins replaced him with a raw-boned first baseman out of Columbia University by the name of Lou Gehrig. The man who would become known as the "Iron Horse" would be in the lineup for the next 2,130 games.

**OCTOBER 10, 1926**—Grover Cleveland Alexander, who won Game 6 and was sleeping off a hangover, is called upon to face Yankees second baseman Tony Lazzeri with the bases loaded in the seventh inning of Game 7 of the World Series. Lazzeri drives a ball into the bleachers that's just foul before striking out against the 39-year-old Alexander. The old warhorse holds on to beat the Yankees 3–2, clinching the championship for St. Louis.

> **OFF THE WALL**
> There are 20 plaques and six monuments in Monument Park. Five of the monuments honor members of the Yankees organization (Lou Gehrig, Babe Ruth, Mickey Mantle, Joe DiMaggio, and Miller Huggins), while a sixth pays tribute to 9/11 victims and rescuers.

**SEPTEMBER 30, 1927**—Just when it appears the Bambino can't raise the bar any higher, he does just that, blasting his 60th home run off Washington Senators' pitcher Tom Zachary to surpass by one the single-season mark he established six years earlier. According to a game story in the *New York Times*, "The Babe made his triumphant, almost regal, tour of the base paths. He jogged around slowly, touched each bag firmly and carefully, and when he embedded his spikes in the rubber disk to record officially homer number 60, hats were tossed into the air, papers were torn up and thrown liberally, and the spirit of celebration permeated the place."

**NOVEMBER 10, 1928**—Top-ranked Army leads Notre Dame 6–0 at intermission, and in an effort to fire up the Fighting Irish, coach Knute Rockne invokes the memory of the school's greatest football hero to that point, George Gipp, who died in 1920. In a story Rockne is believed to have made up, he told of meeting with Gipp on his deathbed. The star player supposedly told Rockne, "Some day, when the team is up against it, and the breaks are beating the boys, tell 'em to go out there with everything they've got, and win just one for the Gipper." The tale may have been apocryphal, but it also proved to be inspiring. The Irish players stormed out of the locker room and went on to upset the Cadets 12–6.

**APRIL 18, 1929**—The Yankees become the first team in Major League Baseball to wear numbers on their uniforms. The numbers basically follow the batting order, which is why Babe Ruth is issued No. 3 and Lou Gehrig, No. 4.

*Two of the most famous Yankees ever, Lou Gehrig (left) and Babe Ruth (right) hold up young Harold Baker at Yankee Stadium on October 7, 1927.* Photo courtesy of AP/Wide World Images.

**MAY 19, 1929**—A cloudburst causes fans in the right-field bleachers to rush for cover, and during the stampede that ensues, two people are killed and 62 others are injured.

**JULY 5, 1930**—The first Negro Leagues game at the stadium attracts 20,000 fans, and the New York Lincoln Giants split a doubleheader with the Baltimore Black Sox.

**SEPTEMBER 27, 1930**—Famed Negro Leagues slugger Josh Gibson crushes a line drive that bangs off the back bullpen wall in left field. The drive by the Homestead Grays catcher is estimated to have traveled 505 feet. Eyewitnesses say if it were two feet higher it would have been the first fair ball hit out of Yankee Stadium. There have been stories about Gibson hitting a ball over the left-field roof during a 1934 game, but they've never been confirmed.

**MAY 30, 1932**—The first monument at Yankee Stadium is dedicated in memory of Miller Huggins, who managed the team from 1918 until his death from blood poisoning in 1929. Interestingly, the granite monument was placed in playing territory, in center field, roughly 450 feet from home plate.

**JUNE 19, 1936**—Joe Louis is an 8–1 favorite to extend his string of knockouts to 23 and his victory streak to 27 on the ring over second base. But in the fourth round, Max Schmeling

*Former heavyweight boxing champ Max Schmeling steps on scale before his historic bout with Joe Louis at Yankee Stadium on June 19, 1936. Louis was the favorite to win, but Schmeling beat him in 12 rounds.*

floors him with a right to the left temple. Louis bounces up after a count of two but is pummeled by more right hands. Louis rights himself, but Schmeling staggers him near the end of Round 5, and the Brown Bomber can barely make it back to his corner. Louis gamely holds on till the 12th round when Schmeling sends him to the canvas once more. Louis tries to get up, but to no avail, and Schmeling is the new heavyweight champion of the world.

**MAY 30, 1938**—A record crowd of 81,841 watches the Yanks beat Boston 10–0 and 5–4 in a doubleheader. Boston's player-manager Joe Cronin and Jake Powell of the Yanks are suspended 10 games each for fighting.

**OFF THE WALL**
New York University played 96 football games at the stadium, more than any other college. Using the ballpark as a secondary home field from 1923 to 1948, NYU posted a record of 52 wins, 40 losses, and 4 ties.

**JUNE 22, 1938**—Joe Louis annihilates Germany's Max Schmeling to reclaim the heavyweight championship crown and debunk Adolf Hitler's mythological theory about Aryan superiority. A crowd of close to 80,000 watches as Louis staggers Schmeling with a one-two combination, and the German boxer goes down for a count of three. Louis smothers him again and then knocks him down for another count of three. Schmeling's cornerman Max Machon waves the white towel through the ropes, and the fight is over just two minutes, four seconds into the first round. Writes historian Roger Wilkins: "Even whites who hated blacks, but were patriotic and despised the Nazis, loved Louis for that."

**AUGUST 27, 1938**—Montgomery Marcellus Pearson throws the first no-hitter in stadium history as the Yankees clobber the Cleveland Indians 13–0. Known to his teammates and opponents as "Monte," Pearson had a brief but extraordinary career for the Bombers, with a 63–27 record and two All-Star Game appearances from 1936 to 1940.

**JULY 4, 1939**—On Lou Gehrig Appreciation Day, the Yankees first baseman says an emotional good-bye to his fans and teammates. His "luckiest man on the face of the earth" speech is regarded as baseball's Gettysburg Address. Gehrig's No. 4 becomes the first jersey in sports history to be retired.

**JULY 11, 1939**—The first of four scheduled Major League Baseball All-Star Games is played at Yankee Stadium. Joe DiMaggio homers as the American League scores a 3–1 victory before a crowd of 62,892. Yankees manager Joe McCarthy wound up starting six of his players for the AL.

**MAY 15, 1941**—Joe DiMaggio launches his famous 56-game hitting streak with a single off Edgar Smith in a 13–1 loss to the Chicago White Sox.

**JULY 4, 1941**—A monument to late Yankees great Lou Gehrig is unveiled in center field, next to the one honoring Miller Huggins.

**OCTOBER 5, 1941**—With two outs in the bottom of the ninth and the Yankees trailing by a run, Tommy Henrich strikes out, but the ball scoots by Brooklyn Dodgers catcher Mickey Owen. Henrich reaches base safely on the passed ball, and the Yankees rally to beat the Dodgers 7–4 in Game 4 of the World Series. What makes the play even more bizarre is that, during the regular season, Owen established a major league record by handling 476 consecutive chances behind the plate without an error.

**MAY 28, 1946**—The first night game is played at the stadium, but the Washington Senators spoil the evening for the majority of the 49,917 spectators by beating the Yankees 2–1.

**SEPTEMBER 27, 1946**—More than 40,000 spectators watch as Tony Zale—the so-called "Man of Steel"—knocks out New York native Rocky Graziano in the sixth round of their middleweight bout.

**NOVEMBER 9, 1946**—Top-ranked Army, featuring Heisman Trophy–winning running backs Doc Blanchard and Glenn Davis, meets Notre Dame in what college football writers dub "The Game of the Century." The teams play to a scoreless tie, snapping the Cadets' win streak at 25 and catapulting the second-ranked Irish to the national championship at the end of the season.

**APRIL 27, 1947**—Babe Ruth pulls on his No. 3 uniform for the last time at Yankee Stadium as part of Old Timer's Day. Ruth borrows the bat of Cleveland Indians pitcher Bob Feller to lean

*Rear view of longtime Yankee Babe Ruth standing in the field at Yankee Stadium on the day his number was retired. Nat Fein won a Pulitzer Prize for this classic photograph.*

on while out on the field. Nat Fein snaps a shot of a withered Ruth from behind, and the memorable photograph earns him a Pulitzer Prize.

**OCTOBER 5, 1947**—During Game 6 of the World Series, stoic Joe DiMaggio shows his frustration on the baseball diamond for one of the few times during his brilliant career. With the Dodgers leading 8–5 and two Yankees aboard, Joe D lashes a 415-foot drive toward the left-center-field bullpen. Brooklyn left fielder Al Gionfriddo, who entered the game that inning as a defensive replacement, races back, back, back to the fence and robs DiMaggio of a game-tying homer. The sensational play prompts Dodgers broadcaster Red Barber to exclaim, "Oh, doctor!" In one of the more memorable images in baseball history, DiMaggio kicks the dirt as he closes in on second base.

**JUNE 13, 1948**—Stricken with throat cancer, a frail Babe Ruth addresses the crowd a final time in a raspy, hoarse voice at the house he built. The Yankees officially retire his number. Sixty-five days later, the Babe dies, and 200,000 fans stream through the concourse at Yankee Stadium to view the slugger's open casket and pay their last respects. Ruth is laid to rest at The Gate of Heaven Cemetery in Mt. Pleasant, New York.

**APRIL 19, 1949**—A monument to Babe Ruth is unveiled next to the ones memorializing Miller Huggins and Lou Gehrig in center field.

**OCTOBER 1–2, 1949**—The Red Sox come to town, having won 59 of their previous 78 games and needing only one more victory to clinch the American League pennant. But the Yankees prove ungracious hosts. They stake the Sox to a 4–0 lead in the first game of the two-game series, but come back to win 5–4 on Johnny Lindell's eighth-inning homer on Joe DiMaggio Day. On the final day of the season, Vic Raschi pitches eight scoreless innings, and the Yanks hold on to win 5–3 and finish atop the American League standings. In the joyous Yankees clubhouse, manager Casey Stengel tells his team: "Fellas, I want to thank you all for going to all the trouble to do this for me." New York goes on to win its first of five consecutive World Series.

**OFF THE WALL**
**Yankee Stadium has been the site of a major league–record three perfect games—Don Larsen (1956), David Wells (1998), and David Cone (1999).**

**AUGUST 2, 1950**—A Yankee Stadium attendance record is established when 123,707 worshippers show up for a Jehovah's Witnesses convention. To accommodate the huge crowd, thousands are allowed to sit on the field. It is the first of several religious conventions to be held in The House That Ruth Built.

**APRIL 17, 1951**—A raw-boned, 19-year-old phenom named Mickey Mantle makes his Yankee Stadium debut. The game also marks the beginning of Bob Sheppard's career as the stadium's longtime public address announcer.

**SEPTEMBER 17, 1951**—Phil Rizzuto's suicide squeeze bunt scores Joe DiMaggio from third base as the Yankees nip Cleveland 2–1 to take control of the pennant race. Indians pitcher

Bob Lemon deliberately threw a high fastball the instant he saw DiMaggio break from third, but Rizzuto somehow managed to get the bunt down. By the time Lemon fielded it, Joe D had scored the winning run, and the disgusted Indians pitcher chucked the ball into the stands.

**SEPTEMBER 28, 1951**—Allie Reynolds throws his second no-hitter of the season as the Yankees shut out Boston 8–0. The most dramatic moment occurs when "the SuperChief" retires Red Sox Hall of Famer Ted Williams for the final out. Reynolds induces Williams to pop up in foul territory behind the plate, but catcher Yogi Berra drops the ball. On the next pitch, Williams pops up to almost the same spot, and this time Berra squeezes it to preserve the gem.

**OCTOBER 5, 1951**—In a play involving three of the greatest center fielders of all time, Mickey Mantle accidentally injures his knee on a fly ball hit by Willie Mays of the New York Giants in Game 2 of the World Series. Mantle, who is playing right field, is told by manager Casey Stengel to take every ball he can get to because Yankees center fielder Joe DiMaggio is nursing a bad heel. Mantle races after the ball hit by Mays leading off the fifth inning, but pulls up when DiMaggio yells, "I got it," at the last second. Mantle's spikes get caught in a wood sprinkler cover and he tears ligaments in his knee—the first in a series of debilitating injuries he will suffer in his starstruck 18-year career.

**JUNE 25, 1952**—On one of the hottest nights in New York City history, Sugar Ray Robinson suffers the first and only knockout of his illustrious boxing career. Joey Maxim is credited with the knockout in that world light-heavyweight bout, but, in reality, Robinson is KO'd by heat stroke rather than Maxim. In his bid to match Henry Armstrong's feat of winning titles in three different divisions, Robinson pounds Maxim incessantly to easily take the first 11 rounds. But, in doing so, Sugar Ray winds up punching himself out in the 104-degree heat. By the end of the $10^{th}$ round, referee Ruby Goldstein succumbs to the sauna and has to be replaced—the only time that has ever happened in a championship bout. And three rounds later, Robinson begins wilting. At the end of the $13^{th}$, he stumbles to his corner and has to be hoisted onto his stool. His cornermen can't revive him, and Maxim is declared the winner.

**OCTOBER 5, 1953**—Billy Martin caps a superb World Series by driving home Hank Bauer with the winning run in the bottom of the ninth of Game 6 as the Yankees defeat Brooklyn 4–3 to capture their unprecedented fifth consecutive Fall Classic. The combative Yankees second baseman rips 12 hits, drives in eight runs, and bats .500 to win Series MVP honors. Whitey Ford strikes out seven and yields just a single run before giving way to Allie Reynolds in the eighth. The Dodgers wind up tying the game with two runs in the top of the ninth, but Martin gets Reynolds off the hook with his clutch hit.

**SEPTEMBER 17, 1954**—Rocky Marciano, the only heavy-weight champion to retire undefeated, almost is beaten by Ezzard Charles. Marciano is bleeding so badly by the eighth round that his cornermen think the fight might be stopped.

**OFF THE WALL**

The longest game in Yankee Stadium history occurred on August 29, 1967, with the Bronx Bombers edging the Boston Red Sox 4–3 in 20 innings.

But as the seconds tick away in that round, Marciano drops Charles with a right cross for a count of four and then chases him across the ring and finishes him off with a left hook and right cross to remain unbeaten. *Ring* magazine names the bout its "Fight of the Year."

**OCTOBER 4, 1955**—"Next Year" finally arrives for the long-suffering residents of Brooklyn as Johnny Podres pitches a complete-game shutout in Game 7 at Yankee Stadium to give the Dodgers their first World Series title. A celebration ensues in Brooklyn that rivals the one marking the end of World War II. The Dodgers had been to seven Series since 1916, including four against the Yankees in the previous eight years, but couldn't find a way to beat them until Podres showed them how. The southpaw from upstate New York wins two games during the Fall Classic to earn MVP honors. The turning point of the Series comes in the sixth inning of Game 7 when Sandy Amoros, a defensive replacement in left field, makes a brilliant running catch of Yogi Berra's opposite-field fly with the tying runs aboard. Amoros whirls and throws to shortstop Pee Wee Reese, who relays the ball to first baseman Gil Hodges to double off Gil McDougald and kill the Yankees rally.

**APRIL 29, 1956**—Four years before he is elected president of the United States, charismatic Massachusetts senator John F. Kennedy delivers an eloquent speech before a crowd of more than 40,000 at a ceremony celebrating the eighth anniversary of the formation of Israel.

**MAY 30, 1956**—Mickey Mantle blasts a 2–2 fastball from Washington Senators' pitcher Pedro Ramos off the decorative copper frieze hanging from the right-field roof at Yankee Stadium. Afterward, Ramos told reporters: "If it had not hit the roof, it would have landed in Brooklyn."

**OCTOBER 8, 1956**—Just two years after posting a putrid 3–21 record with the Baltimore Orioles, Don Larsen is acquired by the Yankees in a 17-player trade and becomes the only pitcher in baseball history to throw a perfect game in the World Series as he blanks the Brooklyn Dodgers 2–0 in Game 5. Larsen is yanked in Game 2, after walking four Dodgers in just one and two-thirds innings and thinks he is through for the Series. But, in a surprise move, Yankees manager Casey Stengel calls upon him again, and on this day Larsen is "pitcher perfect." That's not to say the lanky right-hander doesn't experience a few scares on his way to perfection, because he does. In the second inning, Jackie Robinson lines a ball that ricochets off the glove of third baseman Andy Carey, but shortstop Gil McDougald retrieves it and nips the Dodgers' runner at first base by a step. In the fourth inning, Brooklyn center fielder Duke Snider pulls a deep fly down the right-field line that hooks foul at the last minute. And in the fifth, Mickey Mantle makes a sensational running catch of a Gil Hodges blast to deep left-center that would have gone for extra bases. Mantle's solo homer in the bottom of the fourth winds up being all the run support Larsen needs as he outduels Sal "the Barber" Maglie. Shortly after Larsen completes his 97-pitch masterpiece by getting Dale Mitchell on a called third strike, Yankees catcher Yogi Berra runs out to the mound and leaps into Larsen's arms.

**DECEMBER 30, 1956**—The New York football Giants cap their first season in Yankee Stadium by trouncing the Chicago Bears 47–7, in front of 56,836 fans in the NFL championship game. Fullback Alex Webster rushes for two touchdowns and Frank Gifford and Kyle Rote catch scoring tosses from quarterback Charlie Conerly for the Giants. Featuring seven Pro Bowl players, the Jim Lee Howell–coached Eastern Division champs sprint to a 20–0 lead and never look back. Deafening chants of "DEE-fense! DEE-fense! DEE-fense!" fill the ballpark each time the Bears have the ball. The 12th-man cheers become a tradition at Yankee Stadium and eventually are adopted by fans in football stadiums across the country.

**JULY 20, 1957**—The Reverend Billy Graham hosts one of his crusades at the stadium. More than 100,000—including Vice President Richard Nixon—attend the rally. New York City police estimate that they were forced to turn away another 20,000 people.

**SEPTEMBER 7, 1957**—To commemorate his 25th anniversary as bishop of the Archdiocese of New York, Francis Cardinal Spellman celebrates mass for 50,000 at the stadium.

**SEPTEMBER 23, 1957**—Carmen Basilio upsets Sugar Ray Robinson in a split decision to claim the middleweight championship in front of a crowd of 40,000. The *New York Times* calls it "15 rounds of the most savage fighting at the Yankee Stadium." Basilio, the son of an onion farmer from upstate New York, winds up winning the Hickok Belt as the United States top professional athlete.

**DECEMBER 28, 1958**—In what's still regarded as the greatest football game ever played, the Baltimore Colts, behind quarterback Johnny Unitas, defeat the Giants 23–17 in overtime in the NFL championship contest. Alan Ameche scores the decisive touchdown 8 minutes and 15 seconds into sudden death.

"That was the first game to be nationally televised and the first postseason game ever to go into overtime," said Unitas, who connected with wide receiver Raymond Berry three consecutive times on the drive that led to Steve Myhra's game-tying field goal near the end of regulation. "It got into more households than any other sporting event up to that time. Everything involved with the game served to catch the fancy of the viewing public...it all came together perfectly to make it a great sales promotion for the NFL."

**JUNE 26, 1959**—Ingemar Johansson, an unknown fighter from Sweden, shocks the boxing world by pummeling heavyweight Floyd Patterson. The champ, who entered the fight an overwhelming favorite, is sent to the canvas seven times before Johansson knocks him out for good in the third round.

**JULY 13, 1960**—In the second major league All-Star Game played at Yankee Stadium, Yankees ace Whitey Ford yields home runs to Eddie Mathews and Willie Mays in the first three innings, and the National League cruises to a 6–0 victory in front of 38,362 fans. The victors tie the All-Star Game record with four home runs.

**NOVEMBER 20, 1960**—In one of the most vicious and memorable hits in pro football history, Philadelphia Eagles linebacker Chuck Bednarik nails Frank Gifford just after the Giants halfback catches a pass. Gifford winds up fumbling, the Eagles recover, and Philadelphia goes on to win the game and later the league championship. Gifford is taken off the field on a stretcher and misses the remainder of the season. He decides to retire, he says, not because of the hit, but because he wants to pursue his radio and television broadcasting career full-time.

However, while sitting out the entire 1961 season, Gifford's desire to play returns, and he comes back and plays the 1962–1964 seasons. Bednarik's hit is immortalized on film. The photograph of him pumping his fist over the unconscious Gifford remains one of the most memorable pictures in football history.

**OCTOBER 1, 1961**—A tired and emotionally drained Roger Maris eclipses Babe Ruth's single-season record by clubbing his $61^{st}$ home run

> **OFF THE WALL**
> **Famed public address announcer Bob Sheppard originally turned down the Yankees job when it was offered to him in 1950 because he was afraid it would cut into his teaching schedule.**

off Boston Red Sox pitcher Tracy Stallard in the fourth inning. The ball travels just 360 feet and lands in the sixth row of the lower deck in right field, where it is retrieved by a young man named Sal Durante. After circling the bases, Maris finds his path into the dugout blocked by his teammates. The shy right fielder realizes they aren't going to allow him back to the bench until he acknowledges the crowd. Maris doffs his cap as the 23,154 spectators roar their approval. After the game, the relieved Yankees star tells reporters, "If I never hit another home run—this is the one they can never take away from me." Maris's record would last for 27 years before it was broken by Mark McGwire, who finished with 70. Three years later, Big Mac's mark would be surpassed by Barry Bonds's 73.

**OCTOBER 28, 1962**—Giants quarterback Y.A. Tittle throws for 505 yards and a league-record seven touchdown passes as New York outscores the Washington Redskins 49–34. Giants split end Del Shofner is Tittle's favorite target, shredding the 'Skins secondary for 269 yards.

**DECEMBER 30, 1962**—In what may have been the coldest game in Giants history, New York loses 16–7 to the Green Bay Packers, who ice the win on two Jerry Kramer field goals in the second half. The victory is especially sweet for Packers coach Vince Lombardi, a New York native and former Giants assistant coach who once dreamed of being the head coach of his hometown team.

**MAY 22, 1963**—Mickey Mantle blasts a Bill Fisher pitch off the copper façade hanging from the roof in right field. Just six inches higher and it would have been the first fair ball ever hit out of the stadium. Players and spectators claim it was still rising when it hit the façade. A physicist estimated that the ball would have traveled 620 feet had its path not been impeded. Mantle, the author of numerous tape-measure homers through the years, called it "the hardest ball I've ever hit."

**OCTOBER 2, 1963**—Los Angeles Dodgers' Cy Young Award–winner Sandy Koufax establishes a World Series record by striking out 15 Yankees in Game 1 of the World Series. It breaks the Series single-game record of 14 set by Brooklyn's Carl Erskine during the 1953 Fall Classic. It also sets the tone for a four-game sweep by L.A.

**OCTOBER 4, 1965**—During the first papal visit to North America, Pope Paul VI celebrates mass at Yankee Stadium in front of a crowd of more than 90,000. Before arriving at the stadium, the pope addresses the General Assembly of the United Nations and then meets with President Lyndon Johnson at the Waldorf-Astoria. Nearly 450,000 people requested tickets to attend the mass at the ballpark, which is performed on a wooden stage and altar erected near second base.

**SEPTEMBER 22, 1966**—Only 413 spectators—an all-time low—show up to watch the Chicago White Sox beat the Yankees 4–1. During the telecast of the game, Yankees announcer Red Barber instructs the WPIX cameramen to scan the empty seats for the viewers. The move incenses the Yankee brass, and the Hall of Fame broadcaster is fired after the season.

**MAY 14, 1967**—Mickey Mantle blasts his 500th home run off Stu Miller of the Baltimore Orioles.

**AUGUST 29, 1967**—The Yankees defeat the Boston Red Sox 4–3 in 20 innings—the longest game in Yankee Stadium history.

**JUNE 8, 1969**—A crowd of more than 60,000 shows up for Mickey Mantle Day. The Mick receives a 10-minute standing ovation when Mel Allen calls him from the dugout. After his moving speech, in which he tells the throng that playing baseball in Yankee Stadium is the best thing that could ever happen to a ball-player, Mantle is taken around the warning track in a golf cart and is showered with confetti and applause. The Mick becomes just the fourth Yankee to have his number retired.

**OFF THE WALL**

The stadium's original dimensions were 281 feet down the left-field foul line, 500 feet to left-center, 487 feet to dead center, 429 feet to right-center, and 295 feet down the right-field foul line. Today's dimensions are 318 down the left-field line, 399 to left-center, 408 to dead center, 385 to right-center, and 314 down the right-field line.

**AUGUST 8, 1970**—Hall of Fame manager Casey Stengel makes his first trip back to the stadium since the Yankees fired him following the 1960 season. The "Old Perfessor" receives a huge ovation from the packed house when it's announced that his No. 37 jersey is being retired.

**AUGUST 8, 1972**—The Yankees sign a 30-year lease with the City of New York to play in a remodeled Yankee Stadium, ending speculation that the team might move to New Jersey or Connecticut. The New York Mets agree to allow the Yankees to play their home games during the 1974 and '75 seasons at Shea Stadium.

**SEPTEMBER 23, 1973**—After 17 seasons, the football Giants play their final game at the stadium—a 23–23 tie with the Philadelphia Eagles. The Giants play the rest of their schedule in the Yale Bowl in New Haven, Connecticut, before eventually moving to the New Jersey Meadowlands.

**APRIL 15, 1976**—After the construction firm of Praeger-Kavanaugh-Waterbury completes a two-year, $160 million renovation that removes the roof and façade, as well as the girders that obstructed spectators' views, the "new" Yankee Stadium is unveiled. Bob Shawkey, the winning pitcher in the first-ever game at the stadium, throws out the ceremonial first pitch, and the Yankees go out and beat the Minnesota Twins 11–4. The dramatic changes in the stadium prompt critics to rename the ballpark "The House That John and George Rebuilt" after New York Mayor John Lindsay and Yankees owner George Steinbrenner.

**MAY 20, 1976**—Lou Piniella crashes into Boston catcher Carlton Fisk at home plate, setting off a bench-clearing brawl between the Yankees and Red Sox. Boston pitcher Bill Lee suffers torn ligaments after being slammed to the ground by New York third baseman Graig Nettles.

**SEPTEMBER 28, 1976**—Muhammad Ali, in the twilight of his famed boxing career, turns in a feeble performance but manages to outpoint Ken Norton and hold onto his heavyweight title in the 30th and final championship bout at Yankee Stadium.

**OCTOBER 14, 1976**—Chris Chambliss puts an end to the Yankees' 12-year World Series drought by clubbing a game- and American League Championship Series–winning homer off Kansas City's Mark Littell. The home run prompts thousands of fans to flood onto the field, and Chambliss has to push and shove his way through the chaos in order to reach home plate.

**JULY 19, 1977**—Baltimore Orioles ace Jim Palmer is rocked for five hits and five runs in two innings as the National League scores a 7–5 victory in front of 56,683 fans in the third major league All-Star Game held at the stadium. Los Angeles Dodgers pitcher Don Sutton hurls three shutout innings to earn game MVP honors. An interesting side note: before the game, Yankees and AL manager Billy Martin and baseball's all-time strikeout king Nolan Ryan get into an argument. Martin asked Ryan to pitch in place of the injured Frank Tanana, but Ryan refuses because he believes he shouldn't have been a late addition to the squad. Martin vows to never pick Ryan for an All-Star team again.

**OFF THE WALL**
New York governor Al Smith, who would later run for president of the United States, threw out the ceremonial first pitch before the first game at Yankee Stadium on April 18, 1923.

**OCTOBER 18, 1977**—Reggie Jackson smashes three home runs on three pitches off of three different Los Angeles Dodgers pitchers in Game 6 as the Yankees cap a tumultuous season with a World Series title. The dramatic performance earns Reggie the title of "Mr. October," and he winds up having a candy bar named after him.

**JUNE 17, 1978**—Wiry Yankees left-hander Ron Guidry lives up to his "Louisiana Lightning" moniker by striking out a club-record 18 batters in a 4–0 victory against the California Angels. The game begins the Yankee Stadium tradition of fans clapping when one of their pitchers gets two strikes on a batter. The shutout is one of nine Guidry will throw during his Cy Young campaign, tying the American League record for most white-washings by a southpaw in a season, established by Babe Ruth when he pitched for the Red Sox.

**JULY 29, 1978**—In one of the more bizarre announcements in team history, PA announcer Bob Sheppard tells the fans on Old-Timers' Day that oft-fired Yankees manager Billy Martin will return as the Bronx Bombers' skipper in 1980. As it turns out, Martin winds up replacing Bob Lemon during the 1979 season.

**AUGUST 6, 1979**—On the same day that they buried their captain, Thurman Munson, the Yankees stage an emotional comeback to beat the Baltimore Orioles 5–4. The hero is Bobby Murcer, who had delivered one of the eulogies at Munson's funeral the morning of the game. Murcer wound up driving in all five runs, including the game-winner in the bottom of the ninth. The Yankees continue to honor Munson to this day by keeping his locker intact.

**OCTOBER 2, 1979**—A year after taking over leadership of the Roman Catholic Church, John Paul II becomes the second pope to celebrate mass at the stadium. Nearly 80,000 spectators listen to the Polish-born pontiff talk about the importance of world justice and peace during his two-hour mass.

**JULY 4, 1983**—Dave Righetti throws a no-hitter on the birthday of the United States and Yankees owner George Steinbrenner. It's the sixth regular-season no-hitter in team history and the first since 1951. "Rags" completes the no-hitter against the Boston Red Sox by striking out future Hall of Famer and five-time AL batting champion Wade Boggs.

**JULY 24, 1983**—In what becomes known as "The Pine Tar Game," a home run by Kansas City Royals third baseman George Brett is disallowed after the Yankees protest that the pine tar on Brett's bat extends beyond the legal limit. A furious Brett sprints out of the dugout and has to be restrained while arguing with the umpire crew. The next day, American League President Lee MacPhail rules that the home run stands. Yankees owner George Steinbrenner threatens litigation, but the ruling remains, and the game resumes on August 18. In mock protest, Yankees manager Billy Martin puts pitcher Ron Guidry in center field and left-handed first baseman Don Mattingly at second base. The Royals wind up winning 5–4.

**AUGUST 4, 1985**—Phil Rizzuto Day is held, and the Yankees honor the Scooter by retiring his No. 10 and presenting him with numerous gifts. One of the gag gifts is a cow in honor of the announcer's signature "Holy Cow" phrase. In a humorous moment during the ceremony, the cow accidentally bumps into Rizzuto, knocking him gently to the ground. The day also is significant for another reason—longtime New York Mets star Tom Seaver, then with the Chicago White Sox, records the 300th victory of his Hall of Fame career, beating the Yankees 4–1 on a six-hitter.

**SEPTEMBER 29, 1987**—Don Mattingly establishes a new major league record by clubbing his sixth grand slam of the season to break the mark set by Chicago Cubs Hall of Famer Ernie Banks. Mattingly's blast off of Red Sox pitcher Bruce Hurst in the third inning of a 6–0 victory lands in the third deck of the right-field seats.

**JUNE 21, 1990**—South African freedom fighter Nelson Mandela is welcomed to the United States during a rally at Yankee Stadium. As nearly 80,000 look on, Mandela thanks Americans for their support in the antiapartheid movement. "We knew that our cause would triumph," he says from a stage set up in shallow center field. "We found great comfort in the knowledge that you were with us. Not for a single day did you forget us, not for a single hour." At one point during the celebration, Mandela dons a New York Yankees baseball cap and proclaims to the roaring, appreciative crowd: "I am a Yankee!"

**JUNE 22–23, 1990**—Bronx native and Rock and Roll Hall of Fame musician Billy Joel stages two sold-out concerts at the ballpark. Joel dons a Yankees cap for both performances, introduces his band as if they are the starting lineup of a baseball

*Baseball umpire Joe Brinkman (right) collars Kansas City Royal George Brett in an effort to break up a fight started when Brett was ruled out after using an improper bat during a game against the New York Yankees at Yankee Stadium on July 24, 1983.*

team, and makes references to Babe Ruth, Joe DiMaggio, Mickey Mantle, and other Bronx Bomber greats. Joel brings the house down both nights with soulful renditions of "New York State of Mind" and "Piano Man." Joel returns to the stadium on October

21, 2000, to sing "The Star-Spangled Banner" before Game 1 of the Subway Series between the Yankees and Mets.

**AUGUST 29, 1992**—As part of their Zoo TV tour, the band U2 performs. Singer Bono brings the concert-goers to their feet when he sings the line, "I dreamed I saw Joe DiMaggio dancing with Marilyn Monroe."

**SEPTEMBER 4, 1993**—Jim Abbott, who was born without a right hand, throws a no-hitter in a 4–0 victory against the Cleveland Indians in one of the most inspirational performances in stadium history. The closest the Indians come to getting a hit is in the seventh inning when Yankees third baseman Wade Boggs makes a diving stop of a sharp grounder off the bat of Albert Belle and nips the Cleveland slugger by a step. With the crowd of 27,125 fans on its feet and yelling in the ninth inning, Abbott retires Kenny Lofton and Felix Fermin before inducing Carlos Baerga, the Indians' best hitter, to ground out weakly to short. "I did not know how to act out there [after the final out]," says Abbott, who walks five batters but never allows a base runner past first base. "I didn't know whether to be supremely confident or supremely thankful. I guess it's a little bit of both."

**JUNE 11, 1994**—In what's billed as "The Great Gig in the Bronx," the British rock group Pink Floyd sells out Yankee

*Billy Joel plays for a crowd at Yankee Stadium on June 22, 1990.* Photo courtesy of AP/Wide World Images.

Stadium for a second consecutive night. It's the last time the stadium hosts a rock concert and the final U.S. tour for the band.

**MAY 14, 1996**—Former Mets phenom Doc Gooden, his career derailed by drug addiction, records his second big-league victory in 23 months. And it's a memorable one as he throws a no-hitter for the Yankees against the Seattle Mariners. Adding to the drama is the fact that Gooden's father is scheduled to undergo a double bypass the next morning in a Tampa hospital. It takes Doc 134 pitches to complete the job in front of 20,786 delirious fans. Afterward, the pitcher tells reporters: "This is the greatest feeling of my life. I never thought I could do this, not in my wildest dreams." The 31-year-old Gooden goes on to win 9 of his next 13 decisions to fuel the Yankees during their pennant drive.

**AUGUST 26, 1996**—A monument honoring Mickey Mantle is unveiled in the park just beyond the center-field fence.

**OCTOBER 9, 1996**—The Yankees get by in Game 1 of the American League Championship Series with the help of a 12-year-old. Jeffrey Maier reaches over the right-field wall and deflects a ball hit by rookie Derek Jeter that appears headed into the glove of Baltimore Orioles right fielder Tony Tarasco. Though the television replays show that Maier clearly interfered, the fly ball is ruled a home run. It ties the score, and the Yanks go on to win the game on an 11th-inning homer by Bernie Williams. They also capture the ALCS and win the World Series. Maier's pivotal assist earns him a permanent spot in Yankees lore.

*Baltimore Orioles right fielder Tony Tarasco stretches for the ball as young Yankees fan Jeff Maier deflects it during Game 1 of the American League Championship Series at Yankee Stadium on October 9, 1996. The hit was ruled a home run, tying the ballgame 4–4 in the eighth inning.* Photo courtesy of AP/Wide World Images.

**OCTOBER 26, 1996**—Reliever John Wetteland closes out a 3–2 victory in Game 6 against the Atlanta Braves as the Yankees win their first World Series title in 18 years. Wetteland earns saves in all four victories and is named Series MVP.

**APRIL 13, 1998**—A 500-pound steel joint plunges about 40 feet from the upper deck and crushes a seat. Fortunately, the incident occurs about five hours before a scheduled game, so the stadium is empty and no one is hurt. The Yankees are forced to cancel that night's game against the Anaheim Angels and play several games at Shea Stadium while repairs are made.

**MAY 17, 1998**—Portly southpaw David Wells pitches the 15th perfect game in major league history and the second in team history as the Yankees blank the Minnesota Twins 4–0 in front of 49,820 fans. Just three days shy of his 35th birthday, Wells enters the game with a 5.23 earned-run average, and there is speculation in the newspapers that his spot in the rotation is in jeopardy. But the flaky left-hander feels positive vibes from the ghost of his baseball hero, Babe Ruth, as he strikes out 11 Twins on his way to his perfecto. Right fielder Paul O'Neill gloves the final out, and Wells is mobbed by his teammates and carried off the field. After the game, comedian and lifelong Yankee fan Billy Crystal walks over to Wells in the clubhouse and deadpans: "I got here late. What happened?" The last Yankees perfect game was tossed by Don Larsen, who, in an eerie coincidence, had attended the same high school in San Diego that Wells had.

**SEPTEMBER 25, 1998**—The Yankees win their 112th game of the regular season to establish a new American League record for victories in a season.

**APRIL 25, 1999**—Joe DiMaggio becomes the fifth member of the Yankees organization to have a monument dedicated to him.

**JULY 18, 1999**—To commemorate Yogi Berra Day at Yankee Stadium, Don Larsen, the author of the only perfect game in World Series history, tosses the ceremonial first pitch to Berra. Yankees pitcher David Cone then goes out and tosses the 16th perfect game in baseball history, no-hitting the Montreal Expos.

**OFF THE WALL**
**Late opera star Robert Merrill was a prolific national anthem performer at the stadium.**

**OCTOBER 13, 1999**—The Yankees win Game 1 of the ALCS against the Red Sox on a 10th-inning, walk-off home run by Bernie Williams off of Boston reliever Rod Beck. The game is the first actual postseason meeting between the rivals because the one-game playoff in 1978 technically counted as a regular-season game.

**OCTOBER 21, 2000**—The Yankees score a 4–3 victory in 12 innings against the Mets in the first Subway Series game in New York in 44 years.

**SEPTEMBER 23, 2001**—"A Prayer for America" service sponsored by Oprah Winfrey and James Earl Jones is held to remember those killed in the 9/11 terrorist attacks on the World Trade Center. More than 30,000 people, including former President Bill Clinton and New York Senator Hillary Rodham Clinton, gather at the ballpark. Winfrey, Jones, and New York Mayor Rudy Giuliani are among the speakers. "The Twin Towers may no longer stand, but our skyline will rise again," Giuliani says. "To those who say our city will never be the same again, I say that you are right. I say it will be better." Tenors Placido Domingo and Ronan Tynan perform hymns, the Boys and Girls Choir of Harlem sing "Lift Every Voice and Sing," and singer/actress Bette Midler brings tears to scores of faces with a poignant rendition of "Wind Beneath My Wings."

**OCTOBER 30, 2001**—President George W. Bush becomes the first sitting American president to throw out the ceremonial first pitch at a World Series game in New York since Dwight Eisenhower in 1956. His perfect strike to Yankees catcher Todd Greene before Game 3 against the Arizona Diamondbacks is greeted with chants of "U.S.A.! U.S.A.! U.S.A.!" from the sellout crowd. The Yankees win 2–1 as Roger Clemens allows just three hits and strikes out nine in seven innings.

*"A Prayer for America" was held at Yankee Stadium to honor those affected by 9/11. Oprah Winfrey, Senator Hillary Rodham Clinton, former president Bill Clinton, and then–New York mayor Rudy Giuliani were only a few of the public figures in attendance.*

**OCTOBER 31, 2001**—Derek Jeter hits an opposite-field, walk-off homer in the bottom of the tenth inning as the Yankees defeat the Arizona Diamondbacks 4–3 to knot the Series at two games apiece. Jeter's blast actually occurs shortly after midnight, prompting some sportswriters to dub him "Mr. November," a tongue-in-cheek takeoff on Reggie Jackson's "Mr. October" moniker. The heroics by the Yankee shortstop are made possible by first baseman Tino Martinez, whose two-run homer in the bottom of the ninth sends the game into extra innings.

**NOVEMBER 1, 2001**—For the second straight night a Series game goes into extra innings, and for a second straight night the Yankees rely on extra-inning magic. New York wins it in the twelfth, when Alfonso Soriano singles home Chuck Knoblauch. The most emotional moment of the night occurs when Yankee fans begin chanting Paul O'Neill's name in unison in the top of the ninth. The fiery right fielder is retiring after the Series, and the fans want him to know how much they appreciate his competitive spirit. O'Neill responds by tipping his cap.

**MAY 17, 2002**—Jason Giambi becomes the first Yankee to hit a walk-off grand slam since Babe Ruth in 1925 as New York defeats the Minnesota Twins 13–12 in 14 innings.

**JUNE 11, 2003**—Six Houston Astros pitchers—Roy Oswalt, Pete Munro, Kirk Saarloos, Brad Lidge, Octavio Dotel, and Billy Wagner—combine for the first opponent no-hitter at Yankee Stadium in seven years. It's a major league record for most pitchers combining for a no-hitter and marks the first time the Bronx Bombers have been held without a hit since Hoyt Wilhelm turned the trick on September 20, 1958. The six Houston hurlers allow six Yankees base runners but combine for 13 strikeouts in the 8–0 victory.

**JUNE 13, 2003**—Roger Clemens notches the 300th victory and 4,000th strikeout of his career.

**OCTOBER 16, 2003**—Slumping third baseman Aaron Boone smashes an eleventh-inning, walk-off homer against Boston knuckleballer Tim Wakefield in Game 7 of the American League Championship Series to catapult the Yankees into their 39th Fall Classic. The Yankees come back to tie the game in the eighth inning after Boston manager Grady Little fails to remove a tired Pedro Martinez. The BoSox hurler yields four hits and three runs in the inning, allowing the Yankees to tie the game. Little is canned days later. New York winds up losing to the Florida Marlins in the World Series.

**OFF THE WALL**
The grounds crew dances to the Village People's "YMCA" while changing the bases and grooming the field in the fifth inning.

**OCTOBER 20, 2004**—On what would have been Mickey Mantle's 73rd birthday, the Red Sox defeat the Yankees 10–3 in the final game of the American League Championship Series to become the first team in baseball history and only the third team in major league sports to win a seven-game series after losing the first three games. The Red Sox go on to sweep the St. Louis Cardinals in the World Series, officially ending the 86-year-old "Curse of the Bambino."

**MARCH 10, 2006**—Blind sportswriter Ed Lucas, who has been covering the Yankees for more than a half-century, marries

Alison Pfeifle in the first onfield wedding ceremony at the stadium. Vows have been exchanged in Monument Park and in the stadium banquet venues, but never on the diamond before.

**AUGUST 16, 2006**—A dugout full of dignitaries—including George Steinbrenner, Yogi Berra, Billy Crystal, mayor Michael Bloomberg, and former New York governor George Pataki—attend a groundbreaking ceremony for the new $1 billion Yankee Stadium across the street from the old ballpark. Using commemorative shovels with handles shaped like baseball bats, the celebs turn over the first spadefuls of dirt as construction begins on the new ballpark that's scheduled to open at the start of the 2009 season.

**JANUARY 31, 2007**—Baseball Commissioner Bud Selig announces that the 2008 All-Star Game will be played at Yankee Stadium.

**AUGUST 4, 2007**—Alex Rodriguez becomes the youngest player in major league history to club his 500th home run when he slugs a pitch from Kansas City Royals pitcher Kyle Davies into the left-field seats.

**SEPTEMBER 26, 2007**—The Yankees clinch a spot in the postseason for the 13th consecutive year with a victory against Tampa Bay.

## TENANTS

| | |
|---|---|
| New York Yankees<br>(Major League Baseball) | 1923–1973;<br>1976–2008 |
| New York Yankees<br>(All-American Football Conference) | 1926–1928 |
| New York Yanks<br>(National Football League) | 1950–1951 |
| New York Giants<br>(National Football League) | 1956–1973 |

# 3

# A HOUSE THEY CALL HOME

## A MAN OF TRUE VISION

After more than a half-century, Ed Lucas can still visualize his dad hunkered in front of the family's 12-inch Philco television set, clutching rosary beads and praying for a miracle. And he still remembers jumping up and down in the living room with his father when Bobby Thomson launched the playoff-ending home run that propelled the New York Giants past the Brooklyn Dodgers and into the World Series in one of the legendary moments in baseball history.

"He was screaming and I was screaming," Lucas said, flashing back to October 3, 1951, as if it were yesterday. "We both loved baseball so much. I couldn't wait to get outside and play some ball with my friends."

And within minutes, that's what the 12-year-old boy was doing.

But the ecstasy of the moment would be followed by agony.

On the same day the Giants won the pennant, Lucas would lose his eyesight.

"The Shot Heard 'Round the World" would be followed by "The Shot That Changed Ed's World."

"I threw a pitch to my friend, and he hit a line drive that struck me right between the eyes," Lucas said. "I had bad eyesight to begin with because I was born prematurely and the oxygen buildup at birth had caused my eyes to be weak. The force of the line drive caused hemorrhaging, and it detached my retinas, and I became blind."

Lucas believed he had lost more than just his vision that day.

"I thought my world had ended," he said. "My image of a blind person was someone standing on the street corner with a tin cup and a cane. I was so depressed. I kept thinking, 'What can a blind person do?'"

Lucas has spent the past 57 years answering that question.

Since that life-altering experience as a sixth grader, all he has done is graduate from high school and college, become a sports reporter who's covered the Yankees since the mid-1950s, raise two boys on his own, and inspire everybody he meets.

"People thought I would hate baseball after what happened," he said. "What they don't understand is that baseball took my sight, but it also gave me a life."

And a lot of significant moments in this most remarkable life have taken place at the sport's greatest shrine—Yankee Stadium. His sons—both married and with families of their own—like to joke that they were raised at The House That Ruth Built.

That's why they weren't surprised in the least when their dad mentioned he would like to get married at the ballpark after he proposed to Allison Pfeifle, whom he had been introduced to by Yankees legend Phil Rizzuto.

No one had ever been married on the field at the stadium, but the Yankees made an exception for Lucas. On March 10, 2006, he and Allison were wed at home plate and celebrated with a reception in one of the ballpark's exclusive dining clubs.

As a surprise gift, Yankees owner George Steinbrenner picked up the entire tab.

"From the day I met him when he bought the team in 1973, he's been nothing but a gentleman to me," Lucas said. "The whole organization has, from the players to the managers and coaches to the front office people."

And none of the friendships he made was stronger than the one he had with Rizzuto. His mom took him to meet the Yankees shortstop back in the early 1950s at a New Jersey clothing store where Rizzuto worked in the off-season. The Scooter immediately took a liking to the teenager and invited him and his mom to be his guest at a Yankees game.

"It was the start of an incredible friendship," Lucas said. "Phil may have been a small man physically, but I've never known anyone with a bigger heart."

Rizzuto introduced Lucas to his teammates during his stadium visit and talked to him about pursuing his dreams. Lucas dreamed of being involved in baseball, but he wondered how he could possibly do so if he couldn't see. Then one day he got an idea. Why not interview players on a tape recorder and file features for radio stations and newspapers?

"I knew there would be doubters, so I had to go out there at first and prove myself," he said. "And once I showed people I could do it, I found regular work. People hearing or reading my stories didn't know I was blind, and that's what I wanted to achieve."

He reported on the Yankees while attending Seton Hall University. He also fell in love and got married. But the marriage didn't last, and Lucas found himself facing an even bigger challenge: raising his two young sons, Chris and Edward, as a single dad. With the help of family, friends, and even Yankees employees, he managed to make it all work.

"The stadium was our babysitter," Chris Lucas said in a 2006 interview. "It's Babe Ruth's house, but [to] my brother and I, it's our house as well."

In September of 1979, life tossed Lucas another nasty curve when his ex-wife returned and announced she would seek custody of the boys. A long legal battle ensued, with the case climbing all the way to the New Jersey Supreme Court. Scores of witnesses, including several Yankees employees, testified that Lucas had done a marvelous job raising his sons alone.

The following September, in a landmark decision, Lucas was awarded full custody of his sons. It marked the first time in New Jersey history that a male had won full custody from a female and the first time in United States history that a person with a disability had won full custody from a non-disabled spouse.

"First and foremost, I was happy about that ruling because I loved my boys and I couldn't imagine not having them around," Lucas said. "But I also was thrilled with the decision because I believe it struck a blow for the rights of people with disabilities."

Through the years, Lucas has been heavily involved in raising funds for his high school alma mater, the St. Joseph's School for the Blind. With the help of an annual celebrity golf tournament hosted by Rizzuto, Lucas was able to raise millions of dollars to build a state-of-the-art learning center at the school.

> **OFF THE WALL**
> There's an average of at least one marriage proposal per game on the scoreboard at Yankee Stadium. And about five times a year, someone will call frantically and cancel their scheduled proposal.

In the late 1990s, Rizzuto did Lucas another huge favor when the longtime Yankees broadcaster introduced him to his florist. Pfeifle had lost most of her vision a few years earlier and had become quite depressed. Rizzuto suggested that she give Lucas a call.

"We spent six years on the phone before we actually met," Lucas said. "She's a wonderful lady."

The Yankees spared no expense in making their wedding day special. Lucas's sons shared the role of best man. Guests included director Penny Marshall, who has expressed an interest in bringing Ed's inspirational life story to the silver screen.

"It was very emotional having that ceremony at home plate, right near the spot where Lou Gehrig made his famous speech," Lucas said. "I now know what it feels like to be the luckiest man on the face of the earth."

## THE DIVINE VOICE

When Reggie Jackson was preparing his Baseball Hall of Fame acceptance speech during the summer of 1993, he sought the assistance of longtime Yankee Stadium public address announcer Bob Sheppard.

Wise move.

Who better to help Mr. October than the Voice of God himself?

Sheppard's first piece of advice to the verbose slugger was to slice his speech in half.

"I reminded Reggie that brevity is the soul of wit," Sheppard recalled in his distinctive, resonant tones. "Brevity, when it comes to public speaking, especially on a hot summer's day, also is a way of making friends."

When it comes to endearing oneself to audiences, no one has done it better or longer than Bob Sheppard. The Queens native

*Bob Sheppard, the voice of the New York Yankees, presents his microphone to the National Baseball Hall of Fame and Museum during induction ceremonies on July 23, 2000.*

introduced his first Yankees lineup at the stadium on April 17, 1951, and since that time has worked more than 4,500 baseball games in The House That Ruth Built.

Most New York fans probably wouldn't recognize him if they saw him on the street, but Sheppard's Q-rating among strangers surely would shoot up dramatically the minute he opened his mouth.

His sonorous, dignified voice has become as much a part of stadium lore as the pinstripes on the Yankees uniforms and the copper façade that once hung from the old ballpark's roof. He has been a constant, the man who connects generations of stadium-goers—from Joe DiMaggio to Derek Jeter, from grandpa to grandson and granddaughter.

"I can't imagine a home Yankees game without Bob's voice booming out of the loudspeakers," said Goose Gossage, the legendary Yankees reliever. "I still get chills running up and down my spine when I hear him say my name. You're not officially a Yankee until he announces you that first time. And then when he does, it's like you are connected to all the great players who came before you."

The funny thing is that this six-decade-long gig almost didn't happen. Yankee officials were impressed with the PA job Sheppard had done for two old All-American Football Conference teams—the Brooklyn Dodgers and New York Yankees. So, before the 1950 season, they offered him the baseball job at the stadium, but Sheppard refused because the day games during the spring would interfere with his work as a speech professor at his alma mater, St. John's University.

The baseball club approached him again before the '51 season with a compromise offer. They would find a substitute for him on the days there was a scheduling conflict.

Sheppard accepted, never anticipating that he would still be at the microphone in 2007.

"A temporary job," he quipped, "that has lasted a half-century."

For the record, the first name he announced from his loge-level perch behind home plate that afternoon was that of Boston Red Sox center fielder Dom DiMaggio. Interestingly, Sheppard would say the names of eight players in the starting line-ups at that 1951 home opener who would eventually be honored with plaques at the Baseball Hall of Fame. Among them would be Sheppard's all-time favorite name—Mickey Mantle.

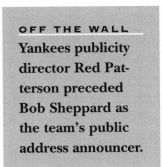

**OFF THE WALL**
Yankees publicity director Red Patterson preceded Bob Sheppard as the team's public address announcer.

"I loved the alliteration of that name and the emphasis you could place on the first syllable of his last name," he explained.

Though best known as the stadium voice of the Yankees, Sheppard also has worked for several other teams and venues through the years. He was the PA announcer for the New York football Giants for 50 years—18 at Yankee Stadium and 32 at Giants Stadium in East Rutherford, New Jersey. And he also worked games at Ebbets Field in Brooklyn and at the Polo Grounds, which was located just two miles from Yankee Stadium across the Harlem River in upper Manhattan.

Long before he began announcing games, Sheppard enjoyed playing them. He was a first baseman and quarterback at

St. John's and played semipro football for $25 a game after graduating from college.

Though he is extremely honored that he has become a part of Yankees lore, he is more gratified by the work he did as a teacher.

"I think teaching was more important in my life than public address because teaching had a greater impact on society," said Sheppard, who continued to work as a professor at St. John's into the 1990s. "I've heard from hundreds of students I taught. The number of ballplayers I've heard from you can count on one hand.

"I'm not into hero worship," continued Sheppard, who is a devout Roman Catholic and a lector at his church on Long Island. "I usually keep my distance from players and managers. And that's as it should be. I have a job to do at the ballpark, and so do they."

He may not have heard from many players through the years, but he can rest assured he made an impact on them. Mantle once told Sheppard he experienced goose bumps hearing the Voice of the Yankees pronounce his name. Sheppard, who delivered a stirring tribute the day Mantle died, told the Mick he had a similar reaction each time he announced the slugger's name.

Mantle was hardly alone in his reaction.

"Nobody—and I mean nobody—has ever said people's names better," said former Yankees third baseman Scott Brosius. "You get the feeling that when it's your time to meet St. Peter at the pearly gates, Bob Sheppard is going to be standing there next to him, introducing you."

Sheppard's favorite Yankee Stadium moments include Don Larsen's perfect game against the Brooklyn Dodgers in the 1956 World Series, Roger Maris's record-breaking 61st homer in 1961, Chris Chambliss's walk-off homer against the Kansas City Royals in the 1976 American League Championship Series, and Jackson's three-homers-on-three-pitches explosion in Game 6 of the 1977 World Series against the Los Angeles Dodgers.

Chambliss's memorable blast was preceded by a stoppage in play because fans had thrown debris onto the field. Sheppard made an announcement telling the unruly spectators to refrain from such behavior. They stopped and the game resumed. When Chambliss homered—ending the game and a 12-year Yankees' World Series drought—thousands of spectators rushed onto the field. This time, Sheppard's mic remained silent.

"The game was over, the Yankees had won, 10,000 people, as if they were shot out of a cannon, ran out on the field, and I just folded my arms and let them do it," Sheppard recalled in a 2000 interview with *USA Today*. "I could never have stopped them. The Marines couldn't have stopped them. Nobody could have stopped them. It had to happen. I never saw anything like it before, and I've never seen anything like it since."

## A CRYSTAL-CLEAR LOVE AFFAIR

May 30, 1956, remains indelibly etched in Billy Crystal's mind.

That was the day the future actor, comedian, and director attended his first game at Yankee Stadium, and Mickey Mantle wound up making quite an impression on the eight-year-old boy and the copper façade hanging from the right-field roof.

During that afternoon contest between the Yankees and Washington Senators, Crystal and thousands of others watched in awe as the blond Bronx Bomber launched a moon shot that barely missed becoming the first fair ball hit completely out of the stadium. Mantle's blast on a 2–2 fastball from Senators pitcher Pedro Ramos ricocheted off the decorative façade, just 18 inches from the top of the roof.

After the game, Ramos joked to reporters: "If it had not hit the roof, it would have landed in Brooklyn."

The Mick's loooooong home run capped an extraordinary day for young Billy—a day that would change his life forever.

His father was a concert promoter who managed the old Commodore Music Shop on 42nd Street in Manhattan. Legendary jazz artist Louis Armstrong had given the elder Crystal his box seats for a Yankees game that late May day, and the father had planned on taking Billy's older brother. But when his big brother hurt his back, the ticket went to Billy. His dad arranged for Yankees trainer Gus Mauch to take Billy down to the home-team clubhouse before the game.

*Comedian Billy Crystal, a lifelong Yankees fan, has the honor of throwing out the first pitch before the Yankees face the Boston Red Sox at Yankee Stadium on May 29, 2005.* Photo courtesy of AP/Wide World Images.

"You can imagine how exciting that was for a little kid," Crystal told the *New York Times* in a 1998 interview. "Gus came out and talked to us and then took my program inside and brought it out with all the signatures on it. [Yankees manager] Casey Stengel came out in the hall, and I remember saying, 'Who's pitching today, Casey?' and he looked at me and said, 'You are, kid, suit up.' How could you not be a Yankees fan after that?"

Mantle became his idol and the stadium the center of his young universe.

Crystal would make the 90-minute trek on the Long Island Railroad to the famed ballpark about 25 times a season after that memorable day. And he and the neighborhood kids in the New York suburb of Long Beach would play baseball in the summers from sunrise to sunset.

Crystal blossomed into an outstanding second baseman and earned a baseball scholarship to Marshall University in West Virginia. But his baseball-playing days ended when the school dropped the program his freshman year.

He wound up returning to the metropolitan area and eventually studied film and television at New York University, where one of his professors was Academy Award–winning director Martin Scorsese.

After working for several years as a stand-up comic, Crystal left Long Island for Hollywood in 1976 and, a year later, got his big break when he landed the role of the gay character Jodie Dallas on the ABC sitcom *Soap*. He later became a regular on *Saturday Night Live,* where his "you look mahvellous" impression of Fernando Lamas became a huge hit with viewers. His career peaked in the late 1980s and early '90s when his roles in blockbuster movies such as *When Harry Met Sally...* and *City Slickers* established him as a major star. His celebrity status only grew when he became a frequent host of the Academy Awards show.

Along the way, Crystal developed a friendship with Mantle, his childhood idol. The Mick said on several occasions if anyone ever did produce a movie about him, he'd want it to be Crystal. And in 2001, six years after the Hall of Fame baseball player died, Crystal debuted the film *61\**, which took a behind-the-scenes look at Mantle and Roger Maris's pursuit of Babe Ruth's home-run record during the historic 1961 season.

Nearly a half-century after his first trip there, Yankee Stadium remains one of the most special places in Crystal's world. Though he lives on the West Coast, he has returned often to the ballpark to watch games and take part in special ceremonies.

The stadium he first saw in 1956 underwent massive changes during the renovations of the mid-1970s, but it still remains a magical place.

"I still feel the same way I did when I was a little boy," he said. "The joy it gave me when I was playing with my friends, pretending to be a Yankee, or pretending with my brother that we were broadcasting the games.

"I just think of my father. Every time I'm [there], I think of my father. I think of the way he got us to love it without saying, 'Love this.'"

## THE OCTOGENARIAN CHEERLEADER

After retiring in 1988 from the trucking business he had founded, Freddy Schuman began searching for something to occupy all the free time he was about to have on his hands. One day, while scanning the sports pages, the 62-year-old Bronx native was shocked to discover that the mighty Yankees of his youth were in last place and that a cone of silence had enveloped The House That Ruth Built.

"I read where the fans had become apathetic and the stadium was no longer an intimidating place for teams to visit," Schuman recalled. "I wanted to do something to wake Yankee fans up and get them back to supporting their team."

Schuman remembered how his mother used to let him and his siblings bang spoons and pots and pans together on New Year's Eve when the clock struck midnight. He believed if he could walk around the stadium during Yankees games beating a spoon against a frying pan, he'd eventually be able to rouse the spectators from their lethargy.

It sounded like a crazy idea, but then Yankees community relations director Dick Kraft decided to let Schuman give it a try.

"He essentially said, 'You can do it as long as nobody complains,'" Schuman recounted.

No one did.

And the super fan known as Freddy Sez wound up beating not only a frying pan, but the odds.

*Yankees fan Freddy "Freddy Sez" Schuman holds his handmade sign in front of Yankee Stadium on October 8, 2006, one day after the Yankees were knocked out of the postseason by the Detroit Tigers in Game 4 of the American League Division Series.* Photo courtesy of AP/Wide World Images.

For the past two decades, the man with the kitchen utensils and the pinstriped Yankees jersey has become a staple at the stadium. The team gives him free admission and free reign, and Schuman takes full advantage of the unlimited access, roaming the upper deck, the loge, and the lower deck during games. Spectators gladly chant, "Let's go, Yankees" with him and often ask him to pose for pictures and sign autographs.

Their biggest kick, though, comes when Schuman hands them the spoon, so they can bang away on his battered, metal frying pan.

"My ego gets so pumped up when they do that," he said. "It makes me feel as if I've made a difference."

He said the slang name "Sez" is a takeoff on a name used by a popular New York City dress retailer from a bygone era. Schuman shows up at the park carrying a cardboard sign bearing different slogans.

He's had many thrilling moments as a super fan, but the tops probably was when the Yankees ended an 18-year World Series drought in 1996. The Bronx Bombers rallied from a two-game deficit in that Series against the Atlanta Braves to win it all in six. Schuman remembers how the fans at the stadium were reenergized when an eight-year-old boy took hold of the spoon during the final game.

"This kid whacked the devil out of the frying pan, and the fans started making noise, and the Yankees scored three runs, and went on to win the game and the Series," he said. "It took a little kid to remind people that a ballpark is one of the few places in society where it's all right to make noise."

Several days after that victory, the Yankees were honored in a ticker-tape parade through New York's "Canyon of Heroes," and Schuman was invited to ride with the players on one of the floats. He also participated in a City Hall ceremony attended by more than a million fans. At one point, Yankees owner George

Steinbrenner took Schuman's spoon and began rapping the pan, but the sound was rather wimpy. New York Mayor Rudy Giuliani asked Steinbrenner to hand him the instrument so he could demonstrate how it was done. To the delight of Schuman and the crowd, Giuliani beat the pan as loudly as Freddy Sez himself.

"That's what it's all about," Schuman said. "I wanted people to feel pride in their team and their city again. It's all about making a little noise and having some fun."

## ANITA'S ASHES

Tom Bartolini first pledged his allegiance to the New York Yankees while growing up in Waterbury, Connecticut, during the late 1940s and early '50s. His passion for the pinstripes was ingrained in him by his Italian-immigrant dad who decided the team deserved the family's unconditional loyalty because the Bronx Bombers had so many paisans with surnames from the old country in their lineup.

Tom's love for the team was reinforced by a jovial neighborhood butcher who would give the youngster a free bag of potato chips each time he answered "Yanks" when asked to name the greatest baseball club on the planet.

Tom vividly remembers his first trip to The House That Ruth Built during the summer of '56. He sat in the mezzanine, and although his view was partially obstructed by the steel girders that held up the ballpark's upper decks and roof, he could barely contain his excitement. The Yankees beat the Cleveland Indians that day on a Joe Collins homer. Tom was hooked for life.

As the years passed, he thought for sure no one could equal his fervor for the Yanks. Then he met his future wife, Anita, and discovered that he had more than met his match.

Anita knew the stats of every Yankees player like the back of her hand. The two were married in 1966, and their love for the Bronx Bombers was surpassed only by their love for each other and their family and friends.

They would listen to games on the radio, watch them on television, and make annual pilgrimages to the stadium from their home in Avon in upstate New York. Like a family heirloom, their love of the Yankees was passed on to their daughter, two sons, and grandchildren.

They festooned one of their rooms with photographs and drawings of the Babe, Joe D., and Thurman Munson and filled shelves with balls autographed by Don "Donnie Baseball" Mattingly, Graig Nettles, and the Goose.

"The Yankees became like an extended member of our family," Tom said. "We scheduled things around their games. I remember one time going to a wedding, and Anita brought a radio with her because the Yankees were playing an important game. Some people scoffed at her at first, but as the evening went on, they kept coming over to see what the score was."

Life was grand for the Bartolinis until the spring of 2000 when they received the horrible news that Anita had terminal lung cancer. The prognosis was that she wouldn't last the summer, but she defied the odds and held on until November 4.

"I truly believe," said Tom, a 61-year-old financial analyst, "that she refused to go until she saw the Yankees win the World Series again."

Before she died, Anita made a tearful request. She asked her husband of 34 years and her three children to have her body cremated and her ashes spread in two places—the Atlantic Ocean near the Connecticut/Rhode Island shoreline where she grew up, and at the stadium.

"We assured her we would do that for her," Tom recalled. "We were too broken up at the time to even think that we might run into a snag."

Tossing Anita's ashes into the sea was a breeze, but spreading them onto the hallowed grounds of her favorite ballpark became as challenging as hitting against Mariano Rivera with a toothpick as a bat. Shortly after her death, friends of her family relayed her desires to the Yankees, only to be told by club officials that ordinances prevented them from allowing someone's remains to be spread in a public place such as the stadium.

"I was disappointed, but I understood why they had those restrictions because I'm sure everybody and his brother would want to do it," Tom said. "They probably would receive so many requests that the stadium would be filled with ashes if they said yes to all of them. And I'm sure it would have been impossible to draw the line."

So Anita's ashes remained in a canister on a shelf in Tom's home until he received an out-of-left-field phone call from his daughter, Erika, one day nearly three years after Anita's death.

"She said, 'Dad, it's time to fulfill Mom's wish,'" Tom recalled. "I told her that we had been through all this untold times before and it wasn't possible, but she said she had a plan."

It called for them to inconspicuously spread her remains during a stadium tour. And that is what they did.

First they headed to Connecticut and tossed some of her ashes into the ocean while reciting prayers specific to Anita's work as a nurse.

> **OFF THE WALL**
>
> **Rock star Meat Loaf wants to have his ashes spread over Yankee Stadium in the middle of the night by helicopter. Many fans request to spread the ashes of loved ones at the stadium, but health codes prohibit it.**

Then they drove to the South Bronx, confident, but not totally certain, that they would be able to accomplish the second part of their mission.

Before leaving for New York, Tom pulled out his camera bag and scooped his wife's ashes into about 10 small film canisters.

"I wasn't thinking about it as a way to get the ashes past security," he said. "I was thinking about what I could put them in so that my kids and their spouses would each be able to spread their mom's ashes where they wanted to."

He had the bag and two cameras strung around his neck, and the stadium security guard thought nothing of it when he inspected the case and saw all the film holders inside it.

"He just figured I was one of those giddy fans—which I was— and that I would be taking hundreds of pictures during the tour—which I did," Tom said.

Before entering the Yankees dugout from the bowels of the stadium, Tom discreetly dispensed the canisters to his kids. They went about their business, quietly spreading the ashes in the dugout, behind home plate, along the third-base line, and near the retired numbers at Monument Park.

"I think the guide may have noticed that something was up, but he kind of pretended that he didn't," Tom said. "He just kept going about his business while we went about ours."

When the tour ended, the Bartolini family and a dozen other tourists were taken to the stadium gift shop.

"The instant we walked in there, we felt a tremendous sense of relief," Tom said. "It was as if all this emotion that had been pent up in each of us for three years had been released. It was such a happy, exhilarating moment because Anita was finally where she had wanted to be, where she belonged."

## THE LION'S DEN AT THE BRONX ZOO

Vinny Milano—better known to friends and strangers alike as Bald Vinny—sat in the right-field bleachers at Yankee Stadium for the first time as a 20-year-old college student back in the summer of 1995.

It took him less than an inning to decide he had the best seat in the house.

Never mind that he and his fellow Bleacher Creatures were nearly 400 feet from home plate and that you couldn't tell the difference between a Roger Clemens fastball and a Tim Wakefield knuckleball from that distance.

Never mind that they were sitting on hard, backless benches and that the beer was overpriced and occasionally as flat as the pitching rubber.

The atmosphere in the cheap seats was more charged than a lightning bolt, and Milano couldn't help but fall in love with the creative, often obnoxious cast of characters who populated section 39. Milano couldn't get over how relentless they were in their attempts to create a home-field advantage for the Yankees. They truly were the Bronx Bombers' 10th man.

In Milano's mind, these were the real fans, as opposed to the corporate types in the suites or the box seats who couldn't tell you if Mickey Mantle or Mickey Mouse once roamed center field at the stadium.

"I said to myself, 'Oh my God. This is the most insane experience I've ever had at a ballgame,'" he recalled. "You sit in the box seats and tell people to get off their asses and cheer, and they look at you like you're from another planet. But out in the bleachers, it's the people who sit on their hands and don't get into the game that are considered strange. This ain't no freaking tennis match. It's a ballgame, and you're supposed to get into it and have fun."

Milano had so much fun at that game that he vowed to never sit anyplace else in Yankee Stadium again.

Which is why, for the past 13 seasons, section 39 has been home for him and other members of the Bleacher Creatures, a group of fans who were given that name by *The Village Voice* and who were immortalized in a book by [New York] *Daily News* sportswriter Filip Bondy.

They have become a tradition at Yankee Stadium, much to the delight of Yankees players, and much to the dismay of security guards and opposing right fielders.

"I've felt their wrath, and I've felt their love, and believe me when I tell you that you are much better off feeling their love," said Johnny Damon, the current Yankees center fielder who experienced their venom when he came to town with the hated Boston Red Sox for several seasons. "Even when I was with Boston, I got a kick out of their creativity. They definitely torture you, but they do so in a clever, intelligent way. I'm just glad they're now on my side."

The Bleacher Creatures have become best known for their top-of-the-first-inning roll call, in which they chant the names of the Yankees' starting lineup. In one of the few interactive cheers in professional sports, each of the players acknowledges the chants with a doff of the cap or a wave of the hand.

"It's just our way to say hello and make them feel like we've got their backs," Milano said.

The Creatures don't stop chanting a name until the player responds. There have been occasions when they've had to repeat a guy's name several times.

"On occasion, Scott Brosius let us keep on going that first year he came to the Yankees from Oakland," Milano said. "He claimed he didn't know that he was supposed to point to us, but we're not buying it. We think he just wanted to hear us chant his name over and over. It was okay because it just allowed us to cheer some more."

The Creatures have their own rules of etiquette. The wave is verboten. So is dancing the Macarena. Cell phones are permitted only for emergencies. Men coming directly from the office are required to remove their ties. And unless you don't mind seeing your regalia torn to shreds or go up in flames, it's best not to show up in an opposing cap or jersey.

*Suck* appears to be one of the Creatures' favorite words—as in Red Sox suck, Mets suck, box seats suck, everybody sucks. The bleacherites tend to be vulgar, but they do prize creativity. They were the ones who started the "nineteen eighteen!" chants in reference to the last time Boston won a World Series before finally ending the "Curse of the Bambino" in 2004.

The Creatures are as much a social group as they are a fan club. Milano said there aren't any official membership cards or dues. The major requirements for inclusion are face time in the bleachers, a knowledge of the game, and a passion for pinstripes.

He said there is a core group of about 75 dyed-in-the-wool Bleacher Creatures, and they go by names such as Bad Mouth Larry, Milton the Cowbell Man, Midget Mike, Nature Boy, Israeli Joe, and Sheriff Tom. They are an eclectic mix of people. The group includes a millionaire, a breast-cancer survivor, victims of 9/11, attorneys, teachers, law enforcement officers, and businessmen.

> **OFF THE WALL**
> Bronx native Tony Morante has been giving tours of Yankee Stadium since Election Day 1979. More than 40,000 people are guided by Morante through the fabled ballpark each year.

"A number of us have developed extremely close friendships," Milano said. "Some of the Creatures stood up in my wedding, and I've stood up in theirs. We have holiday parties. It really has developed into something very special."

For Milano, cheering for the Yankees literally has become a way of life and a livelihood. He had worked several years for a dot-com company. When it went belly-up, he used his severance pay to buy silk-screening equipment and began manufacturing a line of Bleacher Creature wear that has really taken off.

Like his fellow Creatures, he worries about the impact of the switch to the new stadium. In an effort to curb the rowdy behavior in section 39 and adjacent sections, the Yankees stopped selling beer in the bleachers several years ago. And there are concerns that the Creatures might be priced out of the new ballpark because its seating capacity will be reduced by several thousand seats.

"I think it would be a shame if we are kept out," Milano said. "I think we really add to the atmosphere. We like to think we've become part of the tradition there, that we truly are the 10th man, and that we give the Yankees a home-field advantage they definitely would lose if the only people in the stands are the 'suits.'"

# 4

# Yankees Reminisce

## Mickey Mantle

After watching a fleet-footed Oklahoma strong boy named Mickey Mantle wallop several jaw-dropping homers during the 1951 exhibition season, Yankees manager Casey Stengel could barely contain himself. "There's no park in America, not even Yellowstone, that this boy can't hit one out of," Casey boasted to reporters. "And he flies around those bases and across that outfield like a jackrabbit. I've never seen anything like him." Nobody had. Though a series of debilitating injuries and too many nights on the town may have prevented Mantle from reaching his full potential, what he did achieve was none too shabby. In 18 years—all with the Yankees—the Mick slugged 536 homers in the regular season plus a record 18 in World Series play. He won three American League Most Valuable Player awards and led the Yankees to 12 pennants and seven Series titles. The most popular player of his generation, Mantle was inducted in the Baseball Hall of Fame when he first became eligible in 1974. His death in 1995 marked the end of an era for millions of baby boomers.

*Mickey Mantle poses next to his old uniform just prior to the ceremony where his jersey number was officially retired on June 8, 1969.*

"I told the fans when the Yankees retired my No. 7 in the summer of '69 that playing 18 years in front of them in Yankee Stadium was the best thing that could ever happen to a ballplayer, and I meant that.

"I had a lot of thrilling days in that ballpark, and one of the most memorable ones was my first game there in 1951. I remember coming up the steps of the dugout to head out onto the field to take our positions, and I kind of froze. Yogi [Berra] walked over to me and said, 'Kid, you nervous?' And I tried to act cool and tell him I wasn't, and he said, 'Then why you wearing your jockstrap outside your uniform pants?' I laughed at his joke, then ran out to right field as fast as I've ever run before. I'd never seen so many people gathered in one place before in my life. You could have fit 20 of my hometowns in there.

"As I stood in right field, I thought about how I was standing in the same spot where Babe Ruth had. I couldn't help but look every so often to my right and see Joe DiMaggio in center, and then when Ted Williams came to the plate, I couldn't stop gawking at him. Good thing he didn't hit anything to me in that at-bat, because my legs were shaking so much I probably would have fallen on my ass chasing the ball.

"The fans were kind of rough on me in New York for a while because Casey had bragged about me a lot, and when I didn't turn out to be the ballplayer he told them I would be, folks started booing me. It's funny, but they really didn't start coming totally to my side until 1961 when Roger [Maris] and me were locked up in that home-run race. Because I had been there 10 years and Roger had only been there a couple of years, more of the fans started pulling for me. I felt bad for Roger because he was a great ballplayer and a great man. But it sure was nice for me to hear cheers instead of boos for a change.

"I was never one to stand there and admire my home runs the way modern players do because I didn't want to make the pitcher feel any worse than he already did. But there were two occasions when I stayed at the plate a little longer. In 1956 and again in '63 I hit balls that I thought had a chance of going out of Yankee Stadium. Both of those balls hit that copper façade on the right-field roof, and the one in '63 was still rising.

"Hitting that game-winning homer off Barney Schultz of the St. Louis Cardinals in the 1964 World Series was one of my biggest thrills at the stadium because it not only won the game, but it

OFF THE WALL

Sixteen Yankees have had their numbers retired. They are: Billy Martin (1), Babe Ruth (3), Lou Gehrig (4), Joe DiMaggio (5), Mickey Mantle (7), Yogi Berra (8), Bill Dickey (8), Roger Maris (9), Phil Rizzuto (10), Thurman Munson (15), Whitey Ford (16), Don Mattingly (23), Elston Howard (32), Casey Stengel (37), Reggie Jackson (44), and Ron Guidry (49).

broke the Babe's World Series home-run record. That's the only time in my career when I called a home run. Ellie Howard was in the on-deck circle as I was going to the plate to lead off the bottom of the ninth, and I told Ellie he could put his bat back in the rack because I was going to end it right here, and luckily I did. Barney threw a knuckler that didn't knuckle, and I got all of it.

> **OFF THE WALL**
> **Mickey Mantle holds the record for most home runs at Yankee Stadium (266), followed by Babe Ruth (259) and Lou Gehrig (251).**

"Maybe the greatest moment I ever had was when they retired my number. At that time, they had only retired the numbers of Ruth, Gehrig, and DiMaggio. At the end of the ceremony, they took me around the stadium in a golf cart. There were 60,000 people there that day, and I wish I could have thanked each and every one of them personally."

## BOBBY MURCER

Though he never did become the "next Mickey Mantle," Murcer wound up having a stellar big-league career and became one of the most popular Yankees of all-time. The left-handed-hitting center fielder from Oklahoma clubbed 252 homers, drove in 1,043 runs, and batted .277 during a 17-year career that saw him earn All-Star honors five times. He twice hit three homers in a game and tied

the major league record by hitting four homers in four consecutive at-bats. His most memorable performance came on August 6,
1979. In the morning he delivered the eulogy at the funeral of his
friend and teammate Thurman Munson, who had died when the
jet he was piloting crashed. That night, Murcer drove in all five
runs, including the game-winning two-run single in the bottom of
the ninth, as the Yankees defeated the Baltimore Orioles on one of
the most emotional nights in team history. Murcer remained with
the Yankees as a broadcaster after he retired as a player in 1983.
He was diagnosed with a malignant brain tumor around Christmas-
time 2006 and underwent surgery. He returned to the broadcast
booth in time for the 2007 season opener and was on hand for a
number of telecasts throughout the year.

"It was pretty intimidating when I first showed up to Yankee
Stadium as a player. I was still a teenager, and a lot of the writers
and broadcasters were expecting me to be a phenom like Mickey
was when he came up for the first time as a 19-year-old. Rookies
always had to go through a rite of passage. The veterans would
make you carry their bags or they'd make you wait 'til the very
end of batting practice before they'd let you in the cage—things
like that. But my rite of passage wasn't nearly as rough as it could
have been because Mickey took a liking to me, and he was the
unquestioned leader of the ballclub, so everybody else would
take their cues from him.

"I think Mickey remembered what it was like to be a 19-year-
old in that clubhouse like I was, and what it was like to have

people heaping such huge expectations on you. When he came up they expected him to be the next Joe DiMaggio. He knew how hard that pressure could be. Plus I was from Oklahoma, like he was, so he wanted to ease things a bit for a fellow Oklahoman. One day, he put his arm around me in the middle of the club-house and introduced me to everyone, and after that nobody bothered me. He cleared the way for me.

"I've had a lot of great memories at the stadium, but none was more emotional than playing a game the same day we buried Thurman. That was really tough. It wound up being an incred-ible night, but I wished he had never died so we didn't have to experience that. The funeral was that morning in Canton, Ohio, and on the plane ride back [manager] Billy Martin came up to me and told me to take the night off. He said, 'You've been through so much. You're dog-tired. You haven't slept in days, so take the night off.' It was a really nice gesture by Billy, but I told him that for some strange reason, I didn't feel tired. I told him I felt like I needed to play tonight. I wanted to play. And, he said, 'Okay. I understand. If you want to play, then you can play.'

"I realize now that I was operating on nothing but emotion and adrenaline. It was really hard to keep your focus and not think about Thurman. The Yankees did a nice thing by not hav-ing anyone stand in the catcher's position behind home plate during the national anthem. They purposely left it vacant for a few minutes in honor of him.

"I never in my life wanted to play well more than I did that night. I, and the rest of the guys, really felt like we were playing not only for ourselves, but also for Thurman. To come through like I did with the homer and then the game-winning hit meant the world to me. It was such a strange feeling when I got that opposite-field single to win the game. I was happy that I had been able to do this for Thurman and I was sad that he was no longer with us."

## REGGIE JACKSON

He predicted that if he ever played in New York he'd be so big they'd name a candy bar after him—and they did. Jackson capped a tumultuous first season with the Yankees in 1977 by lifting them to their first World Series title in 15 years. And he did it with incredible flair, belting three homers on three pitches off three different pitchers in a Game 6 victory against the Los Angeles Dodgers. Jackson's stunning performance earned him the moniker "Mr. October," and made him a Yankee legend forever.

"It was an exciting time. The last time the Yankees had won the World Series was in '62 with Mickey, Whitey, and Yogi. So it had been a long time coming. I remember the electricity of the city. And I certainly remember the first few months of the year being very, very difficult because of the tension between George [Steinbrenner], Billy [Martin], and me. At one point, I went

*Reggie Jackson bats during Game 6 of the 1977 World Series against the Los Angeles Dodgers at Yankee Stadium on October 18, 1977. Jackson assured the Yankees victory by belting three home runs during this historic game.*

upstairs to ask [Yankees general manager] Gabe Paul to trade me. I was dead serious about wanting to get out, but, fortunately, he refused to listen to me.

"Game 6 was unbelievable. Mr. Steinbrenner had taken a lot of heat for bringing me here, and I remember, after one of the home runs, looking up at him, and pointing to him because, clearly, he supported me through all that time. I remember [former Yankees top executive] Mike Burke sitting behind the dugout. I remember George's Rat Pack, and Liza Minnelli, and Diana Ross. I remember a lot of people. It was a wonderful time.

"I was having a good night that night; I was in the groove. If I got a ball to hit, I was going to hit it out of the ballpark. That's just the way I felt.

"I'll never forget that night, never forget the chants of, 'Reggie! Reggie! Reggie!' when I went out to right field after those homers. I have a very, very special place in my heart for New York, the Yankees, the fans here.

"That night made me a lot more comfortable with myself as a player. I felt like I had reached stardom, if you will. To put it in true Reggie style, I became the player I thought I was. It was a nice feeling because I was the highest-paid player in the game. George took a lot of heat for it, and I finally got the heat off him and off me."

## JIM ABBOTT

The Flint, Michigan, native had many special moments in his baseball career, such as winning the Sullivan Award for being the top amateur athlete in the United States while pitching for the University of Michigan, winning a gold medal at the 1988 Olympics, being selected in the first round of the 1988 Major League Baseball Draft, and winning 18 games while posting an earned-run average of 2.89 for the California Angels to finish third in the 1991 Cy Young Award voting. But none of those special moments can compare to what happened to Jim Abbott on September 4, 1993. For on that day, the pitcher who was born without a right hand reached his baseball summit, throwing a no-hitter for the Yankees against the Cleveland Indians at the stadium. Abbott spent 11 seasons in the majors, posting an 87–108 record and a

> **OFF THE WALL**
> The 1942 Yankees won a franchise-record 18 consecutive home games.

4.25 ERA. He currently works as a motivational speaker in Harbor Springs, Michigan.

"I was awestruck the first time I saw Yankee Stadium. One of my favorite aspects of the stadium is the simplicity of the sign outside: 'California Tonight 7:00 PM.'

"Growing up in Detroit with old Tiger Stadium gave me an appreciation for the old ballparks and their mystique.

"I think I won the first time I pitched there in a long, not very well-pitched game.

"I do not recall having electric stuff going into the no-hitter. I was nervous and anxious to do well because I had struggled so badly against the Indians my previous time out. It was only as the game progressed and the excitement grew that my confidence and stuff began to get better.

"About the seventh inning, you began to absorb the excitement of the fans and sense that something special could happen. I wanted to talk with my teammates as I had done all game, but as the game went on I found there were fewer and fewer people around to talk to!

"Kenny Lofton's bunt attempt came as a surprise, but I loved how the Yankee fans voiced their disapproval. The energy of the crowd and their excitement is the single most indelible impression I have of that day. There is no other feeling in the world quite like being swept up in the building excitement of a no-hitter. It is an amazingly shared experience.

"The ending of the game was indescribable. I remember wanting to be close to Matt Nokes and share the moment. I remember being with my wife trying to call everyone we knew to share the moment. It is a cherished moment that you never forget.

"Yankee Stadium is just different. The mound feels as though it is the center of a very special place. It was an honor to pitch there."

## YOGI BERRA

Arguably the most popular living Yankee, Yogi endeared himself to the fans with his clutch hitting and his way with words. He won three Most Valuable Player awards and 10 World Series championship rings during his Hall of Fame career as a catcher, but he has become even better known for his humorous malaprops. The man with the plaque in Cooperstown also has several sayings in Bartlett's. He gave us: "It ain't over 'til it's over"; "It's déjà vu all over again"; and "Nobody goes there anymore because it's too crowded." For 14 years, Yogi stayed away from Yankee Stadium. Not because it was too crowded, but rather because of the way his firing as manager of the Yankees had been handled by George Steinbrenner in 1985. The Yankees owner apologized to Berra in 1999, and Yogi has been a regular at the ballpark ever since.

"When I came to Yankee Stadium for the first time in 1946 I guess I reacted the same way most people do—I couldn't believe how big it was. And I remember thinking to myself, 'Thank God I'm not a right-handed hitter in this place, because the fences are so deep in left-center.' No wonder they called it Death Valley out there.

"It wasn't too bad in right field. It was really short down the line, something like 295 feet to the foul pole, and I figured if I could pull the ball a lot, I'd be okay.

"The other thing that hits you there is the history and tradition. You know that you are dressing in the same clubhouse and using the same lockers as guys like Babe Ruth, Lou Gehrig, Joe DiMaggio, and Bill Dickey, and all the other great Yankees players that came before you. Then you walk down the hallway and through the dugout and out onto the same field those guys played on. That's pretty special.

"It's hard for me to pick one or two favorite memories because I was blessed to have so many good ones there. Heck, I played in 14 World Series and we won 10 of them, so I got a lot of things to choose from.

"Maybe the most memorable game I played in was when Don Larsen threw his perfect game in the 1956 World Series. It's only been done once in the history of baseball. You can't top that, only equal it. Larsen had the best control he ever had in that game. I'd put my glove up, and he seemed to hit the target every time. He got a couple of breaks, too, which you need. Duke Snider hit a long fly ball down the right-field line that would have been a home run if it didn't hook foul at the last min-ute. And Gil Hodges hit a long drive to left-center that would have been a home run in Ebbets Field, but Mickey [Mantle] made a great running catch.

> **OFF THE WALL**
> **A ball hitting either of the stadium foul poles on the fly in the 1930s was not ruled a home run; it was in play.**

"It's funny how so many special things happen at that ball-park. They had me and Larsen back for an anniversary of his no-hitter, and then David Cone goes out and throws a perfect game. That stuff seems to happen at Yankee Stadium more than it does at other places.

"It was tough staying away [for 14 years], but Yankees owner George Steinbrenner came to my museum [in 1999] to apolo-gize for the way he fired me as manager. He said all the right things. I'm glad it's over. It's been great to be back.

"It'll be a sad day when they tear it down. But they'll never be able to tear down the memories."

## CHRIS CHAMBLISS

The sweet-swinging Yankees first baseman is remembered for his quiet leadership during the tumultuous Bronx Zoo era of the late 1970s and early 1980s and for hitting one of the most memorable homers in postseason history. Chambliss's blast off Kansas City's Mark Littell in the bottom of the ninth inning of the final game of the 1976 American League Championship Series snapped the Yankees' 12-year World Series drought and set off the rowdiest postgame celebration in stadium history.

"People still love talking about it, especially when I'm back in New York to visit. And I enjoy reliving it with the fans. Heck, I'd rather be remembered for something like that homer than something bad that happened in my career. It definitely was one of the crazier nights at the stadium. And you had a feeling as the game progressed that it might come down to the end.

"Some people had thrown debris on the field, so there was a delay before I stepped into the batter's box while the maintenance people picked it up. It was a cold October night, and Littell didn't throw during the delay, so he might have stiffened up a bit and it might have affected him mentally, too, because it upset his rhythm. So I guess you could say our home-field advantage might have come into play a little bit.

"I had a feeling it might go the instant I hit it. I was just hoping it had enough height to get over the wall. I never expected the fans to flood onto the field as rapidly as they did. It was like a human tsunami. By the time I reached second it was scary. For a second I was thinking I might not make it around the bases, that maybe I should just make a beeline to the dugout. I had to dodge and bull my way through the people. It was absolutely crazy. You could tell it had been a long time since they had something like this to celebrate and they weren't going to wait a second longer than they had to. Security had no chance of stopping them. I'll obviously never forget the emotion of that night. My only regret is that I didn't get to celebrate with my teammates at home plate the way you see guys do today."

## WHITEY FORD

Four decades after tossing his last pitch in the big leagues, Ford remains the Yankees' "Chairman of the Board" as far as pitching is concerned. The crafty left-hander from Queens tops the franchise charts in victories (236), strikeouts (1,956), and shutouts (45). An eight-time All-Star and winner of the 1961 Cy Young Award, Ford was at his best in the Fall Classic. He established World Series records for wins (10) and consecutive scoreless innings (33⅔). He was inducted in the Hall of Fame in 1974 with his longtime friend and teammate, Mickey Mantle. It was the same year the Yankees retired his No. 16.

"I went to the stadium a couple of times as a kid to watch Joe DiMaggio play. Bleacher tickets were something like 25¢ apiece, and it was a great place to sit because you got the same view on the ball off the bat that DiMaggio got.

"I don't really remember being too much in awe when the Yankees brought me up in July of 1950. Casey [Stengel] threw me out there a lot, and I went 9–1 down the stretch, and we wound up sweeping the Philadelphia Phillies that October.

"Being a left-hander, I thought it was a great place to pitch. People talk about that short porch in right, but it never bothered me because I always had success against left-handed batters. I made 'em hit it straight away or to the opposite field, where there was a lot of room to work with. I knew how to use the park to my advantage. I'd see DiMaggio and Mantle hit so many fly balls to Death Valley. It really was tough on guys batting right-handed. DiMaggio must have lost about 300 homers because of the deepness of the fences. And Mickey lost an awful lot, too.

"October made it even tougher on the hitters because you'd start getting the afternoon shadows rolling across the field. The batter's box would be in the dark and the pitcher would be in the sun, and it would be tough for the hitter to pick up the ball coming out of the sunlight and into the darkness of the shadow.

"One of the most memorable games I ever saw there was Larsen's no-hitter. I actually watched it from the right-field bullpen. Don had gotten rocked in an earlier start in the Series, and Casey didn't know how long he'd last in this start, so he told me to stay loose out there because the instant Don got into trouble, he was going to call on me. Obviously, the bullpen phone never rang."

## SCOTT BROSIUS

The third baseman's career with the Yankees was brief (four seasons) but memorable. The Yankees were hoping his solid glove would shore up their defense when they acquired Brosius from the Oakland A's before the 1998 season. It did, and Brosius's lively bat from the lower part of the batting order proved to be a bonus that helped propel the Yankees to the most wins (125, including postseason) in baseball history. Brosius had his most productive offensive season in '98 with 19 homers, 98 RBIs, and a .300 average. He capped the year by winning MVP honors in the Yankees sweep of San Diego in the World Series. Brosius played on three championship teams with the Yankees and played a role in the team's dramatic comeback in Game 5 of the emotional 2001 Series against Arizona with a two-out, two-run homer in the bottom of the ninth.

"I grew up in Oregon, and I remember watching the Game of the Week on Saturday mornings, and those games seemed like they always involved the Yankees. So I guess you could say I became familiar with Yankee tradition at an early age. I remember coming here with the Oakland A's for the home opener in 1997 and watching all the festivities going on. I recall watching from the dugout and saying to myself, 'Man, that would be really cool to be a part of something like that.' And the next year I was.

"I really believe the Yankees organization feeds off its special tradition. No organization knows how to celebrate past successes better than the Yankees, and I think that effort sets an example for the players and teams that follow. I know it was that way with me. I wanted to do something so we could become a permanent part of that tradition, and I think we did by winning three World Series in a row.

"Even in 2001, when we lost in seven games to the Diamondbacks, I think we added to the tradition. Because of what happened on 9/11, that certainly made that Series the most emotional one I've ever been involved in. For us to come back and win Games 4 and 5 in extra innings boosted the city's spirits, gave them a little something to feel good about in a time of such great sadness.

> **OFF THE WALL**
> **Nearly 200,000 streamed through the concourse at Yankee Stadium to pay their respects and view Babe Ruth's coffin in the days following the legendary slugger's death on August 17, 1948.**

"I think one of the biggest things that makes Yankee Stadium so special is the fans. They are so knowledgeable and passionate. I think that roll call by the Bleacher Creatures in right field is so cool. People don't believe me, but I really didn't know why they kept calling my name the first time I took the field for the Yankees at the stadium. Derek [Jeter] had to tell me that they wanted me to tip my cap and acknowledge them. Some people think I would let them keep chanting my name just to have some fun. Now, why would I do that?"

## DEREK JETER

He grew up in Michigan but spent summers at his grandparents' house in New Jersey. And that was a good thing because it gave Derek Jeter an opportunity to catch his favorite team—the Yankees—on television and radio, and occasionally in person at the stadium. Like thousands of others, Jeter dreamed of one day playing for the Bronx Bombers, and his childhood fantasy came true. A decade into his career, he has four World Series rings and has established himself as the greatest shortstop in franchise history. By the time he's through, he should hold the records for most hits and most games played in a Yankee uniform. Like Ruth, Gehrig, DiMaggio, and Mantle before him, he has become the face of his Yankees era.

"To me, I have the greatest job in the world—shortstop for the New York Yankees. And I get to go to work at the best office in the world—Yankee Stadium. It's an honor to work there, and I never forget that. I love the history that comes along with the job. I really believe when you are playing for the New York Yankees, you are playing for all the guys who came before you and all the guys who are going to follow you. And that's a pretty big responsibility.

"We have the best fans in the world. They're knowledgeable and they're passionate. They cheer you on and they keep you honest. They have high expectations, and I like that because I do, too. That's the way it should be.

*Fans react as New York Yankees shortstop Derek Jeter dives into the stands for a ball during the Yankees' 5–4 victory against the Boston Red Sox on July 1, 2004, at Yankee Stadium.* Photo courtesy of AP/Wide World Images.

"There's a sign hanging in the runway leading from our clubhouse to the dugout. It's a quote from Joe DiMaggio thanking the Lord for making him a Yankee. I look at that sign every home game I head out to the field. I feel the same way."

## TONY KUBEK

On his father's advice, Kubek turned down scholarship offers to play football at Notre Dame and Michigan and signed with the Yankees organization. Kubek's dad had played professionally, and he believed his son would be able to climb the ladder rapidly and take over for an aging Phil Rizzuto at shortstop. Father knew best. Kubek showed up at Yankee Stadium as a 20-year-old in 1957 and wound up hitting .297 to earn American League Rookie of the Year honors. After a nine-year career with the Yankees, Kubek retired to become a broadcaster. He worked as a color commentator on NBC TV's *Game of the Week* for 24 seasons, and when the network lost the rights to Major League Baseball telecasts, Kubek spent the 1990–1994 seasons broadcasting Yankees games for the Madison Square Garden Network.

"I was too scared to have any emotions the first time I walked onto the field at Yankee Stadium. Actually, at first I was so focused on where I was playing, what the pitcher threw, etc., that I wasn't awestruck. It really wasn't until after I got settled into a routine a few games later that it began to hit me. One day I'm out there, and I realize that Mickey is behind me in center field and that Yogi is behind the plate and Whitey's on the mound. And then you start thinking not only about the legends you are playing with, but also the fact that Babe Ruth and Lou Gehrig and Joe DiMaggio had played on this same field.

"When I think of special times I had there, I think a lot about winning pennants and World Series. And I also have a lot of memories of playing with Mickey Mantle and the incredible things he was able to do. I was there in 1963 when he hit the home run that almost left the stadium. It bounced so hard off the façade in right field that the ball bounced back almost to second base.

"I remember doing a Toronto Blue Jays game at the stadium. Before the game, Buck Martinez and Garth Iorg came up to me and told me, 'You should have seen the shot Fred McGriff hit yesterday,' and they pointed to a spot high in the upper deck. They asked me if I had ever seen anybody hit one farther, and I said Mickey had. And they said, 'No way.'

"Billy Martin was managing the Yankees at the time—no, I don't remember which time—but I knew Billy had this huge photograph showing Mickey at the plate with this dotted line showing the flight of the ball he hit in '63. I asked Billy if I could borrow it to show the guys on the Blue Jays, and he said, 'Sure.' When I brought it over to Buck and Garth and some of the others, their jaws dropped. End of discussion.

"I was a left-handed hitter, and you'd think I'd be happy because the old stadium had the short porch in right. But that was only to your advantage if you were a dead-pull hitter, which I wasn't. Roger Maris wasn't, either, until he became a Yankee. He was no fool. He worked at it and worked at it and worked at it until his stroke became tailor-made for the stadium. Yogi and Johnny Blanchard also were able to perfect their strokes. But I remained more of a straightaway hitter.

"Of course, the old stadium dimensions were brutal if you were a right-handed hitter. I was broadcasting games for NBC, and I remember Dave Winfield was complaining how unfair it was because it was 420 feet to the power alleys in left-center. I told him, if you think it's unfair now, you should have seen how unfair it was in the old stadium when it was 457, 460 feet to that power alley.

**OFF THE WALL**

**The 1961 Yankees set the franchise record for most home victories in a season with 65.**

"When we played the Milwaukee Braves in the World Series in 1958, I remember talking to Henry Aaron after he had reached second base. He said to me, 'How can you guys hit in this place? It's 1,000 feet to the fence, and with all those people in the center-field bleachers and the shadows here in day games, it's hard to pick up the ball.' Then, in 1961, we played the Cincinnati Reds in the World Series, and the great Frank Robinson reached second base, and he said almost the same thing. He said, 'This place is not fair to hitters.' I said, 'Now you know how Joe DiMaggio and Mickey Mantle feel.'

"One time, Mickey hit a ball over Jimmy Piersall's head that went over the monuments that were in play in center field. It was well over 450 feet, and Mickey wound up with an inside-the-park homer. Piersall was a character, so the next time Mickey came up to bat, Piersall positioned himself behind the monuments. Later, he joked that he was having a conversation with Babe Ruth."

## GOOSE GOSSAGE

One of the most feared relief pitchers of all-time, Gossage spent 22 seasons in the big leagues and posted Cooperstown-worthy numbers: 310 saves, 124 wins, and nine All-Star Game selections. Like Mariano Rivera, Gossage was at his best in the postseason, recording a 2–1 record, eight saves, 29 strikeouts, and just seven walks in 31⅓ innings. Three times he led the American League in saves and was named the Rolaids Relief Pitcher of the Year in 1978.

"The first time I pitched in the stadium was in '72 when I was a rookie with the Chicago White Sox. Even though I had grown up in Colorado, I was a huge Yankees fan because my dad had always followed the Yankees. He passed along his love for them to me. I remember shaking in my shoes when I took the mound that first time. My legs were like spaghetti. I was scared to death. My father had passed away a few years earlier, and I remember looking up in the sky and saying, 'Dad, I'm here. I'm at Yankee Stadium. This is for you.' My big thrill, though, came several years later when I was traded to the Yankees. When I took the mound wearing the pinstripes, that was a dream come true.

"I played for nine teams in my career, so I've been to every park in the big leagues, and there's no place like Yankee Stadium. The minute you put on those pinstripes and take that field, you feel the tradition of all the great players who played there, and you feed off the incredible energy of the fans. Yes, they are incredibly demanding because expectations there are so much higher than they are anyplace else, but I loved that. To me, that's the way it should be. The fans at the stadium always held you to a high standard, and that made you better.

"Winning the World Series and adding to the tradition was a huge thrill among many thrills here for me. We had great teams. I'd put our teams of the late 1970s against any of the great Yankee teams. We had some gamers.

"For one game, I'd put the Ron Guidry from 1978 up against any pitcher who ever lived. He went 25–3 and had electric stuff every single start. I still don't know how he wound up losing three games. All I know is that when Gator was slated to start that year, I knew I was going to have the night off. He didn't need any closer that season because he closed out the game himself.

"Probably the strangest game I've ever been involved in at the stadium was the 'Pine Tar Game.' People forget that I was on the mound when George Brett hit that disputed homer. I was the maddest guy in the ballpark when he hit that one out. But after Billy Martin had the umps check the pine tar on Brett's bat and they disallowed the homer, I wasn't so mad any more. When George came storming out of that dugout, I thought for sure he was going to clock one of the umpires.

"When I was playing, one of my favorite days of the season was Old-Timers' Day. You got to share the locker room with many of the guys you grew up idolizing. It was great listening to them tell stories. Now, the current guys are listening to old-timers like me.

It's going to be sad to see the team move across the street. I just can't imagine this place being gone. I don't even want to think about that."

## BOBBY RICHARDSON

A seven-time All-Star and five-time Gold Glove award–winner at second base, Richardson anchored one of the best defensive infields in Yankees and baseball history. His most memorable defensive play occurred in the bottom of the ninth inning in Game 7 of the 1962 World Series, when he caught a screaming line drive off the bat of San Francisco slugger Willie McCovey with the tying and winning runs on base. The catch ended the game and preserved a 1–0 victory. Richardson did damage with his bat in the 1960 Series. Though the Yankees lost to the Pittsburgh Pirates in seven games, Richardson was named MVP after driving in a record 12 runs.

"I signed as 17-year-old, right out of high school in 1953 and I was given a 4-day trip to New York to work out with the Yankees at Yankee Stadium. I took the train from Sumter, South Carolina, to New York, stayed in the Hotel New Yorker, and took a cab out to the stadium. I remember going into the clubhouse, and I was told to put on a uniform and go out and take batting practice and field some grounders before the game with the regulars, then come back in and change back into my street clothes and watch the game from the stands. I recall putting on my uniform, but I didn't put my cleats on because they had carpeting in the clubhouse and I didn't think you were supposed to put your spikes on in there. One of the coaches, Frank Crosetti, laughed at me when he saw me, this wide-eyed teenager, in my stocking feet. He said, 'Kid, put your shoes on. You can walk on this carpet with your cleats.'

"I ventured down the hallways and through the dugout, and I remember being awestruck the instant I saw the stadium. It was so mammoth, and I couldn't help thinking that you could fit about five Sumters in this place.

"I sauntered out near the batting cage, and I was really nervous because I saw Hank Bauer and Yogi Berra and Moose Skowron—guys whose bubblegum cards I had in a shoebox back home. All of a sudden, I feel this arm on my shoulder. It's Mickey Mantle himself, and he says reassuringly, 'Come on, kid, step in there and take some swings.' Each of the four days I was there, Mickey would offer me those same words of encouragement. Well, I can't tell you how big that was for me. Here was the leader of the Yankees putting me at ease and sending a message to all the other regulars that it was okay for this kid to take his swings because one day he might be our teammate. To this day, that act of kindness he showed me remains my most vivid memory of Yankee Stadium.

"One of those days that I was there, they had me on the Yankees pregame television show. I remember the host asking me, 'Son, how long do you think it will be before you'll be coming back to the stadium for good?' I don't remember what I told him, but two years later I was called up to fill in for Gil McDougald, who'd been injured by a line drive. I was only up for about 20 days before they sent me back down, but even though I was there for a brief time, the players wound up voting me a one-third share from the World Series that year. That was extremely generous, and I kind of believe that Mickey was behind that. He probably said, 'Listen, this kid needs some money. Let's give him a piece of our winnings.'

"One of my biggest thrills was when they held a day in my honor back near the end of my career in 1966. At that time, there had been only 10 such days like this, so I was extremely honored. They gave me a lot of nice gifts in the pregame ceremony, and I wanted so badly to pay the team and the fans back with a good day, but it didn't happen. We were playing the Minnesota Twins, and Jim Kaat was

**OFF THE WALL**
**On July 20, 1965, Mel Stottlemyre became the first pitcher in 55 years to hit an inside-the-park home run. It occurred in a 6–3 victory against the Red Sox in the stadium and matched the feat of Pittsburgh Pirates pitcher Deacon Phillippe back in 1910.**

pitching. Jim's a very special friend of mine, and after the Twins got out to a pretty solid lead, he started feeding me fastballs. He was just throwing it right in there for me, but, try as I may, I was unable to get a hit and wound up 0-for-5. Jim and I still laugh about it. I joked to him that I would have been better off if he had tried to get me out."

## DON LARSEN

This much is certain: Don Larsen has to be the most famous 81–91 pitcher of all time. His mediocre career, which included a 3–21 mark in 1954 for the Baltimore Orioles and stints with seven different ballclubs, would have been long forgotten had he not done what he did on October 8, 1956. On that day, in Game 5 of the 1956 World Series, Larsen achieved what no other player ever has—perfection in the Fall Classic. Twenty-seven Brooklyn Dodgers up. Twenty-seven Brooklyn Dodgers down. A no-hitter, a perfect game by the unlikeliest of men—a character known to his teammates as "Gooney Bird."

"I've been asked about it every single day of my life since. People ask me if I ever get bored talking about the same game over and over, and I tell them, 'Why would I get tired of talking about something like that?'

"I'd had some control problems when I started Game 2, and I thought that would be it for me for the rest of the Series. If Casey [Stengel] was going to use me it would be out of the bullpen. I didn't know I'd get another start until I arrived at my locker the day of Game 5. The Yankees had a ritual where [third-base coach] Frank Crosetti would put a brand new baseball in the spikes of that day's starting pitcher. When I got there that morning, the ball was in my left shoe. Yeah, I was nervous. I tried to gulp, and it felt like I had an apple in my throat.

"I went 1-2-3 in the first, then had a scare in the second when [shortstop] Gil McDougald picked up a ball that bounced off our third baseman, Andy Carey, and nipped Jackie Robinson by a step. Jackie was in the latter part of his career and had lost a step or two. Had that been the Robinson of three years earlier, he would have beaten it out for a base hit.

"Later, Duke Snider hit one off me pretty good but it hooked foul or it would have been a homer. And Mickey [Mantle] made a great catch on a long drive to left-center by Gil Hodges. I don't think any other center fielder in baseball could have gotten to that ball, but Mickey could run like a deer. It would have been a homer in any other park. It definitely would have been a homer in the modern Yankee Stadium. That thing would have landed in Monument Park.

"In the latter innings, I went up to Mickey and said, 'Slick, wouldn't it be something if I threw a no-hitter in the World Series?' He told me to f*ck off. Nobody wanted to talk to me because of the superstition that you didn't talk about such things while they were unfolding. I didn't believe in that baseball tradition of jinxing a no-hitter. I just wanted to lighten things up a bit, but my teammates didn't want to have anything to do with me.

"A lot of people forget that Sal Maglie was pitching a great game for the Dodgers, too. We were only leading 2–0, and there were a lot of dangerous hitters in that lineup. The outcome hadn't been decided by any means.

"After I got Dale Mitchell on that called third strike to end the game, I was numb. It wasn't until later that I realized it had not only been a no-hitter, but a perfect game.

"I think it's kind of neat that I have connections to the two other perfect games thrown by Yankee pitchers at the stadium. David Wells attended the same high school in San Diego that I did. And I was there for David Cone's perfect game in 1999 because they had asked me to come in that day to honor Yogi and throw out the ceremonial first pitch.

"As Cone's game got into the late innings, I started feeling nervous like I had back in '56. I knew what kind of pressure he was under and how lonely it gets on the bench."

## GRAIG NETTLES

A superb-fielding third baseman with a sweet left-handed stroke tailor-made for the short right-field porch at Yankee Stadium, Nettles spent 11 seasons with the Yankees. His best season was 1977 when he finished second in the American League in home runs (37) while driving in a career-high 107 runs and winning a Gold Glove. He was the league's leading home-run hitter the previous season with 320. Nettles was one of the most competitive players in Yankees history, and one of the most combative. He tangled with several opposing players while with the Yankees, his most infamous moment coming in a bench-clearing brawl with the Red Sox when he knocked pitcher Bill Lee out for the season. He finished his career with 390 homers, 1,314 RBIs, and a .248 batting average.

"We had some crazy times there—that's why we referred to Yankee Stadium as the Bronx Zoo. When I was there in the 1970s, early '80s, you never knew what was going to happen when you showed up for work. George [Steinbrenner] was always doing something to get Billy [Martin] in a foul mood, and Reggie [Jackson] couldn't keep his mouth shut, and the tabloids ate it all up. That's why I came up with that line: 'Some kids dream of joining the circus, others dream of becoming a baseball player. As a member of the New York Yankees, I have gotten to do both.'

"Hey, but it all worked out in the end, with us winning those back-to-back world championships. We may not have always gotten along away from the field, but between the foul lines we were damn tough to beat. I think we would have matched up well against the modern-day Yankees. We had great clutch players like Thurman [Munson] and Chris Chambliss and Reggie. We had Sparky [Lyle] and Goose [Gossage] in the bullpen. And our starting rotation, with guys like Gator [Ron Guidry] and Catfish [Hunter] and Ed Figueroa, wasn't too shabby. Bring it on. We would have held our own.

"I'm most proud of the fact we brought the winning back to the Yankees. When I got here, you heard a lot about how they had won throughout the '20s and '30s and '40s and '50s and early '60s. George reminded us a lot about the drought, and he put his money where his mouth was and put together a team that brought the glory back to the Bronx.

"There were so many great games I had the privilege of being involved in. I'll never forget that 18-strikeout game by Guidry against the Angels in '78. I didn't get much work that day. It was like he and Thurman were playing catch, and the rest of us were just there to watch. It was like that barnstorming softball team, The King and His Court. There were a lot of games like that for Gator that summer. I've never seen a guy dominate as many games as he did that season.

**OFF THE WALL**

**The Metallica song "Enter Sandman" is played whenever closer Mariano Rivera jogs in from the Yankee Stadium bullpen.**

"For me, my favorite moment probably was when Chambliss hit the home run to put us in the World Series in 1976. That's my number one thrill. I didn't know if he was going to be able to make it through the crowd and be able to touch home plate. I thought he might just make a beeline for the dugout. I wouldn't have blamed him. That scene was scary because those fans were nuts.

"I always loved playing there. Being a left-handed batter, I got my pull swing down really good and learned how to take advantage of that short porch. I'm going to miss that place. She was awfully good to me."

## BOB TURLEY

He was nicknamed "Bullet" because of his blazing fastball, and Turley's heater came in handy during the 1958 World Series, as he won two games and saved another to propel the Yankees to the championship in seven games versus the Milwaukee Braves. The performance capped a sensational season in which Bullet Bob went 21–7 with a 2.97 earned-run average and six shutouts. Known for his no-windup delivery, Turley won the Cy Young Award and the 1958 Hickok Belt as America's top professional athlete. The 6'2" right-hander went 82–52 in his eight seasons with the Yankees.

"The first time I set foot in here was with the Baltimore Orioles, and I beat them 2–1. I remember the bottom of the ninth in particular. Mickey [Mantle] hit a high fly ball to right field, and Cal Abrams caught it leaning against the fence.

"I had a number of memorable games here with the Yankees. I pitched the [World Series] game after Don Larsen threw his perfect game in 1956 and got beat by the Brooklyn Dodgers 1–0. I set a Yankees Series record that still stands by striking out 14 batters, and I scattered just three hits, but we lost when Enos Slaughter misjudged and came charging in, and the ball went over his head, allowing Jackie Robinson to score the only run of the game.

"One of the biggest games I ever pitched came in the 1958 Series when I shut out the Braves. Casey Stengel then called on me to come out of the bullpen in Game 7 in Milwaukee. I pitched six strong innings, and we won the game and the Series.

"On days when I wasn't starting, I'd sit in the dugout and help our hitters by telling them what pitch was coming. I was pretty good at picking up on a pitcher's mannerisms, so we came up with a system where I would whistle to our batters to let them know what they could look for. I know Mickey [Mantle] really appreciated it.

"Watching Mickey play in his prime was a sight to behold. People talk about his long home runs, but pitchers were more afraid that he might hit one back through the box and kill them. When he wasn't hitting the ball 450 feet, he was hitting bullets through the infield. It was shocking how hard he could hit a ball.

"I was there for a couple that he hit off the façade in right. When they took that façade down during the renovations in the 1970s, I'm sure they found some dents in there from balls Mickey hit. Fortunately, it hit that copper rather than some poor guy's head."

## DR. BOBBY BROWN

A dependable third baseman, Brown spent parts of eight seasons with the Yankees in the late 1940s and early '50s, batting .279 with 22 homers in 548 regular-season games. He was one of those players who took his game to another level when October rolled around, as evidenced by his .439 batting average in 17 World Series games. Brown was a part of four Yankees teams that won it all.

Brown roomed with catcher Yogi Berra. It was a strange pairing because Brown was studying to become a doctor while Berra had little formal education. The two reportedly were reading in their hotel room one night—Berra a comic book and Brown a copy of *Gray's Anatomy*. When Yogi finished his comic, he asked Brown, "So, how is yours turning out?"

Brown wound up receiving his medical degree from Tulane University and practiced cardiology in the Dallas–Fort Worth area until the early 1980s when he took over as president of the American League.

"The stadium we played in, well before the renovations of the early 1970s, was gigantic. For the big games, you could easily seat 72,000 fans, nearly 20,000 more than you can now. The field itself was vast, too. A lot of guys, especially the right-handed power hitters, hated to play here because it was 463 feet to left-center. But I absolutely loved it because I was a line-drive hitter and I felt like I had a lot more room to hit the gaps than I had in other ballparks, like Fenway, where the left fielder and center fielder could really play in on you and take away base hits. The outfielders had so much more ground to cover in Yankee Stadium. They were more spread out, and if you did hit one between them, it would roll forever.

"It could be hard to hit here sometimes during game days because they sat people in the center-field bleachers, and if they were wearing white and light-colored shirts, you had a tough time picking up the ball coming out of the pitcher's hand.

"I guess the biggest reason I loved playing here is that we won a lot more times than we lost. What made it great was all the great ballplayers we had. Everybody rooted for one another. We didn't have big arguments. There weren't any fights. It was just a wonderful atmosphere. The architecture of this place was great, but winning is what really made this ballpark special.

"The renovations changed it quite a bit. The fences were brought way in, but it's basically the same place. It's still the 'Home of Champions,' and I still get a tingle every time I walk into Yankee Stadium."

## MICKEY RIVERS

He often walked as if he had 90-year-old knees, but when it came time to chase down fly balls in center field or set the table for sluggers like Reggie Jackson and Thurman Munson, Mickey Rivers was Mick the Quick. He was a catalyst for the Yankees championship runs in 1977 and '78, batting .326 and .265 with on-base percentages of .439 and .397 those seasons. Rivers's sense of humor and his occasional butchering of the English language endeared him to teammates and fans. Before one season, he proclaimed his goals were "to hit .300, score a hundred runs, and stay injury-prone." He asked a teammate: "What was the name of the dog on Rin Tin Tin?" Of his relationship with Yankees owner George Steinbrenner, he once said, "He understands me. Me and him and Billy [Martin] are two of a kind."

"Even though we were known as the Bronx Zoo, we had a lot of fun playing ball back in the '70s. Yeah, we had our battles, but what family doesn't? When it came time to get down to business, we got down to business.

"We definitely had a lot of different personalities on those teams and a lot of ego guys. Reggie [Jackson] could really be a pain at times. He liked to brag on himself quite a bit. One time we're on the team bus and he's bragging about how smart he is. He's going on and on, and I'm getting a headache. When he started talking about how he had an IQ of 160, I couldn't take any more. I said, "'One hundred sixty? Out of what? A thousand?'

"Reggie came in and thought he was the team. But he was okay once we convinced him he was part of the program and not the whole program.

"I really liked Billy. Me and him, we had a good relationship. I felt sorry for him because everywhere he went he had a bull's-eye on him. I remember being in elevators with him, and total strangers would come up and say, 'Hey, you're Billy Martin, aren't you? Wanna fight?'

"I loved playing in Yankee Stadium. The fans were always into it, especially in the bleachers. I loved those cats. I was just glad they were on my side. I felt sorry for the outfielders on the other teams because our fans could be brutal. They definitely gave us an advantage."

## MOOSE SKOWRON

Years before Yankee Stadium fans performed "Moose" calls for pitcher Mike Mussina, they serenaded first baseman Moose Skowron with those primal chants. A former quarterback at Purdue University, Skowron became a fan favorite in the Bronx, earning All-Star honors six times (five times as a Yankee) during a career that saw him hit 211 homers, drive in 888 runs, and bat .282.

"I was a right-handed batter, so this wasn't a great place for me to hit in. The fences were so damn far away. There were times when we couldn't wait to go on road trips so we could hit a few into the seats.

"I was a dead pull hitter when I came here, and one day Casey Stengel pulled me aside and said, 'Moose, if you don't learn how to hit the ball to right field, you are going back to the minors.' So I learned, and I found out it was a lot easier to punch home runs to that short porch in right. I can understand why Joe DiMaggio would get frustrated at times. I'm told he used to get really mad because he'd hit the ball 450 feet to left-center field for an out, and Yogi [Berra] would wrap the ball around that 295-foot foul pole in right for a cheap home run.

"Other than that, I have no complaints about playing here. How could I? Look at the Hall of Fame players I played with here—Mickey [Mantle], Yogi [Berra], and Whitey [Ford], and look at how the fans treated us. I was in New York nine years, and we won seven pennants. You get spoiled. We came to the stadium expecting to win, and we usually did."

## GENE MICHAEL

The lanky, good-fielding, light-hitting shortstop known as "Stick" has worn numerous hats for the Yankees through the years. He's played, managed, and worked in the team's front office. He was a player at the end of Mickey Mantle's career and for the beginning of Thurman Munson's career. He managed Reggie Jackson and helped develop Derek Jeter, Bernie Williams, and Mariano Rivera.

"I was always a sure-handed fielder, but the first time I played in Yankee Stadium you would have thought I never fielded a baseball before. I remember going out for a pop-up that was over my head—a play I had made thousands of times before—and I was so nervous I almost dropped it. Fortunately I set-

**OFF THE WALL**
**Pope Benedict XVI is scheduled to celebrate mass at the stadium in 2008.**

tled down, and we won 1–0 behind Mel Stottlemyre's pitching.

"I guess some of my best moments as a player involved my defense. I helped us win a few games by pulling off the hidden-ball trick and catching a base runner sleeping at second base. I was pretty good at it, and I think I could probably have done it 10 times. But you have to pick your spots because it's embarrassing to the base runner, and he might make you pay the next time he comes chugging down second base trying to break up a double play. That's why I usually tried to pick on someone smaller than me."

## WILLIE RANDOLPH

A native New Yorker, Randolph experienced the Yankees as an All-Star second baseman and as a coach before heading crosstown to become manager of the New York Mets.

"When I think back to my years with the Yankees, I would have to say the highlight for me was the 1977 season. The year before we had been swept by the Cincinnati Reds, so it was a pretty embarrassing offseason. We came into spring training in '77 really motivated to redeem ourselves. We had a lot of turmoil that season with Reggie and Billy and George, but we worked through it and wound up winning it all. That also was the season when I got to play all nine innings of the All-Star Game at Yankee Stadium. That was pretty special to be able to do that in my hometown in front of my family and friends. There's only been a few New York–born players to go on and win a championship with the Yankees. That group included guys like Lou Gehrig and Phil Rizzuto. To follow in their footsteps and to experience that in your hometown is pretty special."

## CLIFF JOHNSON

Although he spent just parts of three seasons with the Yankees, the 6'4", 225-pound Johnson contributed to the 1977–1978 championship teams by providing pop off the bench. Nicknamed "Heathcliff" by Yankees announcer Phil Rizzuto, Johnson clubbed 20 homers and drove in 56 runs in 160 games for the Bombers. He also will be remembered for getting into a clubhouse fight with Goose Gossage that sidelined the Yankees reliever for several weeks.

"We didn't always get along like the best of friends in the locker room or away from the field, but when it came time to play baseball, we were all business. I can remember times when Thurman [Munson] would be scowling and Reggie [Jackson] would be ticking people off, but we put all that aside by the time that first pitch was delivered.

"I wasn't here long, but this stadium was the place to be. You felt like a gladiator in that ancient Roman stadium when you took the field at Yankee Stadium. Something comes over you when you play here, it really does. It's like it transforms you into a different person. In '77 and '78, you could really feel it. There was an energy here like no other place."

## AL DOWNING

A fireballing left-hander, Downing grew up just 60 miles from the stadium in Trenton, New Jersey. He became the first African American to become a member of the Yankees rotation and was one of their aces from 1963 to 1967. Gifted with a 95-mph fastball, Downing posted 13 wins in each of his first two seasons and led the American League in strikeouts in 1964 with 217. Downing's best season came in 1971 with the Los Angeles Dodgers when he went 20–9 and led the NL in shutouts with five. Despite winning 123 games and posting a very respectable 3.22

earned-run average in 17 seasons, Downing is best remembered for delivering Hank Aaron's record-breaking 715th home run early in the 1974 season.

"The first game I pitched at the stadium was against the San Francisco Giants in the old Mayor's Trophy exhibition game back in '61. I had started a game in Washington, but this was different. This one was going to be in front of my family and friends, and I was going to face a lineup that featured [Willie] Mays, [Willie] McCovey and [Felipe] Alou, so I was pretty nervous. I wound up pitching about six innings and gave up just two or three runs, which wasn't bad considering who I was facing.

"I remember coming here three times as a kid. I couldn't believe how big the place was. Television doesn't prepare you for the scope and size of the place. Then, when I came here to pitch for the first time, it looked even bigger than it had when I was in the stands.

"The starting pitchers used to warm up near the dugouts back then, and I felt like that was a pregame advantage for me. I could really bring it and I knew the guys in the other dugout could see and hear how hard I was throwing, so I thought that was a way of sending a little message beforehand, plant a few seeds of doubt in their heads.

"I loved pitching here. My strategy was simple. Because it was really short down both lines, I wanted to keep the ball more toward the middle of the plate and make them hit it straightaway or to the gaps. I knew those would be easy outs because I had a lot of room to play with out there, and I knew with Roger [Maris] in right, Mickey [Mantle] in center, and Tommy [Tresh] in left, I was going to be in pretty good shape because those guys all covered a lot of ground."

## MIKE FERRARO

Although he was voted the Yankees' top minor league player in 1966, Ferraro's big-league playing career never amounted to much. He batted .179 and .161 in parts of two seasons with the Yankees and finished his major league career with just two homers, 30 RBIs, and a .232 batting average while playing for three different teams. He did spend nine seasons as a coach with the Bombers. Ferraro probably is best remembered for incensing George Steinbrenner when he waved home Willie Randolph in the 1980 ALCS against the Kansas City Royals and the Yankees' second baseman was thrown out at the plate. The Yankees wound up losing the series, and Steinbrenner demanded that manager Dick Howser fire Ferraro. When Howser refused, Steinbrenner fired both him and Ferraro.

"When I was a kid growing up in Kingston, north of the city, my dad would take me to the stadium on Saturday so I could see Joe DiMaggio play. But the player I grew up idolizing was Mickey Mantle. I was one of those kids who mimicked everything Mickey did—from the way he ran to the way his knee sometimes buckled when he swung hard from the right side and missed. I had his mannerisms down so perfectly that years later, when I was running the fantasy camp he and Whitey sponsored, I would do imitations of Mickey for the campers, and Mickey would get a kick out of that.

"Unfortunately, I never had the ability that went with those mannerisms. Still, it was quite a thrill when they called me up in 1966, and I got to play with Mickey and Elston Howard and Whitey—guys I grew up idolizing.

"When they brought me back as a coach in the 1980s, they asked me to coach third base. I had been a minor league manager, and minor league managers usually coach third base, so I guess they figured my experience would be a plus. I never realized, though, how scrutinized I'd be. The guy [Steinbrenner] really puts a microscope on you. But that just comes with the territory.

"My baseball-playing career might not have amounted to much, but I can always say I got to play with some of the best players of all time, and I got to play and coach at the greatest ballpark there ever was."

## JOE ALTOBELLI

A journeyman major league player, Altobelli played at the stadium several times while with the Cleveland Indians and Minnesota Twins. He spent two seasons as the Yankees' third-base coach in the early 1980s and later managed against the pinstripes while guiding the Baltimore Orioles to their last World Series title in 1983.

"I never got the same feeling in any other ballpark that I did in Yankee Stadium. I was a left-handed hitter, so being in the same batter's box that Ruth and Gehrig had been in was really special. Then years later, when I stepped into that coaching box at third base, I thought about how Frank Crosetti had been there forever. I think he still has the record for the most World Series rings if you combine the ones he won as a player and a coach. You definitely feel the history there. How can you not?

"It was a nice short porch in right. It was really close, and the fence out there was only about three feet high. The problem is the scouting report would have them pitch you away so left-handed hitters could rarely take advantage of it. I remember coming in for a game in 1961 with the Twins, and I went with the pitch perfectly and I wound up driving one past Mickey Mantle in center field that rolled between the monuments. I'm no speed demon, but I had hit it so far that I wound up with a triple.

"Knowing how fast he was and how much ground he could cover, I thought he might catch it, but I got just enough of it to get it by him.

"I always enjoyed coming there as a manager because you could feel the history there, and guys always played hard there because they knew this was a special place where a lot of great things happened and if you did something great there it had a better chance of being remembered."

## MARTY APPEL

He began his career with the Yankees answering fan mail for
Mickey Mantle and wound up handling media relations for the
franchise when the team was acquired by George Steinbrenner
during the early 1970s. Appel was around for the Bronx Zoo
era, when the Yankees were the winningest and most contro-
versial team in baseball. In his book, *Now Pitching for the Yankees: Spinning the News for Mickey, Billy, and George*, Appel gives
a humorous and poignant look at the Yankees during those
never-a-dull-moment times from the perspective of a front-
office insider.

"I worked in one of the most hallowed places in all of sports,
and there wasn't a single day when I didn't think about that driving to work. Although they had been dead for years, Babe Ruth
and Lou Gehrig were there every day for me. I could feel their
presence.

"When the team was on the road, the members of the Yankees' off-the-field family—the front-office workers, the grounds-
keepers, electricians, painters, security guards, etc.—often would
sit out in the stands and eat lunch. Early in my first year there,
I ventured out to the monuments. One day at lunchtime, I
grabbed a fungo bat and tried to hit a ball over the fence so I
could say that I knew what it was like to hit a home run at Yankee Stadium. It took me several swings, but I finally got one over
the left-field fence. Of course, by the time that happened, I had
moved from home plate to the outfield grass.

*George Steinbrenner, here enjoying having Yankee Stadium all to himself, made it a point not to meddle with Yankees tradition.*

"I was there for the last game in the old stadium in 1973, the last season before they renovated it. That game was made more historic by the fact Ralph Houk resigned as manager immediately after the game. When the final out was made, people literally started uprooting seats and walking out of the stadium with them. You would have thought you were at a garage sale or a scavenger hunt. It actually was kind of sad to see.

"I was working for Bob Fishel when they retired Mickey's number in 1969. Bob did a fabulous job choreographing that ceremony—everything from the World Series pennants being spread on the field to Mickey's ride around the stadium on a golf cart. I've never seen a better ceremony for a player than that one. It went off like perfection.

"Working for George certainly was an experience. He never fired me like he did others. But he did call me into his office about five times a day to tell me he was doing me a favor by not firing me.

"One of the things I do like about George is that he didn't tinker with Yankees tradition. He could have put names on the back of the uniforms or even changed them completely to produce more revenue streams, but he didn't. And I thought the renovations to the stadium in the mid-1970s were done tastefully. I think the new place maintained the majesty and still gave you the feeling of being in the most sacred ballpark in the world.

"It's tough for a lot of us traditionalists to see the old ballpark be replaced. But I think it's perfectly appropriate what they are doing because the current place wasn't built to accommodate 4 million fans a year. To be honest, it's just not a fan-friendly experience when you have to wait half an hour in a concession or men's room line.

"The toughest thing about the move is that you'll no longer be able to point to a spot in the upper deck and say, 'That's where Mickey parked one.' Hopefully, they'll be able to create some new memories. It's just going to take some time."

## HOWIE KARPIN

The Bronx-born Karpin is in his ninth year as full-time official scorer for the Yankees. He also is the author of *Yankees Essential*. He made his first trip to the stadium as a kid in 1965. Though the Bombers lost to the Minnesota Twins 1–0, Karpin was hooked. He was the scorer when a major league–record six Houston Astros pitchers combined to throw a no-hitter at the stadium on June 11, 2003.

"Roy Oswalt got hurt after the first inning and had to come out, which meant the Astros had to cobble together a bunch of relievers to handle the next eight innings. Because there was a new pitcher seemingly every inning, I didn't really notice their staff had a no-hitter going until about the seventh inning. I knew they had Octavio Dotel and Billy Wagner available for the eighth and ninth innings, so I'm thinking, 'Boy, they have a really good chance to pull this off.'

"Sure enough, Dotel comes in for the eighth and winds up striking out four guys because Alfonso Soriano reached first base on a wild pitch on one of the strikeouts. Then Wagner came in for the ninth and retired the side 1-2-3.

"The other interesting part of this game is that I'm the only official scorer in major league history to name the winning pitcher in a no-hitter because in all the other combined no-hitters the starter went five innings to pick up the win. According to the rule book, if the starter doesn't go five innings and the team has the lead, the official scorer has to choose who's awarded the win, and usually it's the pitcher who's most effective. I determined that guy was Brad Lidge, so he was the winning pitcher in probably the strangest game I've ever scored.

"It was the first no-hitter thrown against the Yankees in 45 years, which kind of added to the pressure. I had scored an error against the Astros earlier in the game that was a no-brainer. The tension really mounted in those final innings. You're always praying that, if there's going to be a hit, it's a clean one.

"Two days after the no-hitter, I scored Roger Clemens's 300th victory, so that was some week.

"I've also worked three World Series games at the stadium. I had Game 4 of the 2001 Series when Derek Jeter won the game with a walk-off homer. That was the game that began on Halloween and actually ended on November 1, which is why people were referring to Derek as Mr. November. And I also had Game 2 of the 2000 Series. That was the Subway Series between the Mets and Yankees when Roger Clemens picked up the barrel of Mike Piazza's broken bat and threw it at him. There was nothing in the rule book on how to score that play."

## HARVEY GREENE

A native New Yorker, Greene is in his 19th season as vice president/media relations for the Miami Dolphins. Before joining the NFL franchise, he spent nearly four seasons as the Yankees director of media relations.

"Early in my first year as PR director [1986], I found out that some of our guys used to take early batting practice around 3:00 PM or so, long before the gates opened. I was in the clubhouse one day and some of the players said I was welcome to shag some fly balls during that early session—in fact, they welcomed people in the outfield retrieving the balls hit out there, so I changed into some Yankees warm-up gear, grabbed a glove, and headed to the outfield.

"It was an amazing experience. I was standing in the outfield, the same place where Ruth, DiMaggio, Mantle, and so many other greats enshrined in Monument Park right behind me used to roam. I was shagging balls hit by Dave Winfield, Don Mattingly, etc., and shooting the breeze with some of the players (mostly pitchers) hanging out there. I would catch some fly balls, misjudge and drop others, and basically had a great time out there. Growing up in New York and going to so many games at Yankee Stadium in my youth, I never ever dreamed something like this was possible.

"After a while, I sought more difficult challenges and wandered down to third base. Winfield, a right-handed hitter as tall as a mid-Manhattan skyscraper, was in the cage, and when he saw

## STADIUM NO-HITTERS

Going into the 2008 season, there had been a total of 11 no-hitters tossed at Yankee Stadium—eight by Yankee pitchers and three by opposing hurlers.

Three of the no-no's were perfect games, which is a Major League Baseball record for most perfectos in a single ballpark.

The most memorable of these gems was Don Larsen's perfect game against the Brooklyn Dodgers during the 1956 World Series. It remains the only no-hitter in the history of postseason play.

David Wells (1998) and David Cone (1999) are the authors of the Yankees' other perfect games.

The most bizarre no-hitter in Stadium history occurred on June 11, 2003, when six Houston Astros pitchers combined to blank the Yankees 8–0. Roy Oswalt started the game and Billy Wagner closed it out.

Technically, you could claim there were 12 no-hitters if you include the fictitious one actor Kevin Costner threw in the movie *For Love of the Game,* which was filmed at Yankee Stadium following the 1998 season. Costner played an aging Detroit Tigers pitcher, who saves his best performance for the final game of his illustrious career.

## No-Hitters by the Yankees

| DATE | PITCHER | SCORE | OPPONENT |
| --- | --- | --- | --- |
| August 27, 1938 | Monte Pearson | 13–0 | Cleveland |
| September 28, 1951 | Allie Reynolds | 8–0 | Boston |
| October 8, 1956 | Don Larsen | 2–0 | Brooklyn |
| July 4, 1983 | Dave Righetti | 4–0 | Boston |
| September 4, 1993 | Jim Abbott | 4–0 | Cleveland |
| May 14, 1996 | Dwight Gooden | 2–0 | Seattle |
| May 17, 1998 | David Wells | 4–0 | Minnesota |
| July 18, 1999 | David Cone | 6–0 | Montreal |

## No-Hitters Against the Yankees

| DATE | PITCHER | SCORE | OPPONENT |
| --- | --- | --- | --- |
| April 30, 1946 | Bob Feller | 1–0 | Cleveland |
| August 25, 1952 | Virgil Trucks | 1–0 | Detroit |
| June 11, 2003 | Roy Oswalt, Pete Munro, Kirk Saarloos, Brad Lidge, Octavio Dotel, and Billy Wagner | 8–0 | Houston |

me at third, his eyes lit up, and he started to smile. Sure enough, he hit me a few easy grounders but then started to take a harder swing at the BP offerings. It wasn't long before balls were rifling past my head, stinging line drives that threatened to decapitate me if I didn't duck in time. He finished by hitting a vicious, one-hop missile that skipped right in front of me and would have hit me square in the chops if I hadn't hit the ground.

"As I got up, dusted myself off, and scurried back to the safety of the outfield, Winnie broke up laughing and yelled at me, 'Hope you learned your lesson.' I sure did. Although I continued to come out often for early BP, I never ventured out of the outfield again."

## CHRISTOPHER GRANOZIO

A graduate of Le Moyne College, Granozio has spent more than 10 years operating the sound systems and video boards at a number of New York City sports venues, including Yankee Stadium.

"I have so many stadium memories—such as playing 'New York, New York' with pride from the audio booth after the Yanks swept the Braves in '99, or working both historic day-night, split-venue Subway Series. But the one that may best capture my time in the Bronx was the game during which I predicted a triple play. It was May 29, 2000—Memorial Day—and Major League Baseball had mandated all home teams observe a moment of silence the first inning break after 3:00. The Yanks were batting in the sixth and had runners at first and second with no outs. At 2:58 PM, Legendary PA announcer Bob Sheppard turned to me and spoke through the partition: 'Well, I guess we'll do the announcement after this half-inning.' To which I replied: 'Unless, of course, there's a triple play, Mr. Shep.'

"The very next pitch, Shane Spencer lined to Randy Velarde, who turned an unassisted triple play. The only one ever accomplished in the history of New York City baseball. As soon as Velarde completed the stunning play, Sheppard turned to me with his mouth agape and began applauding."

# 5

# OPPOSING PLAYERS REMINISCE

## CAL RIPKEN JR.

The Yankees rolled out the red carpet for the Baltimore Orioles legend during his final trip to Yankee Stadium on September 30, 2001. They held a pregame ceremony in which Don Mattingly presented Ripken with a pin commemorating his last game in New York and a framed copy of the commemorative ticket that read, "Farewell Cal Ripken" and featured pictures of the Orioles shortstop and Lou Gehrig, the Yankees great whose consecutive-games-played streak was broken by Ripken. During his pregame speech, Ripken told the crowd: "I know there will be many things that I'll miss about baseball, but coming to New York and playing in Yankee Stadium will always be at the top of that list. As a fan of baseball, you realize the history of baseball—period—is very rich, but Yankees history is a very big part of that history. Just being able to walk out here is an awesome feeling. By playing on it for the last 21 years, you begin to realize why it's special. The atmosphere is special." After speaking, Ripken signed autographs for fans and then threw out the ceremonial first pitch to Yankees shortstop Derek Jeter.

It is believed to be the only time an active opposing player was asked to perform those duties.

"I have so many great memories there. I remember my last game there ended in a tie. We played a bunch of extra innings in the rain, and the umpires finally called it. It seemed like it would never end.

"Yankee Stadium is the best place in the world to play when you are good and the Yankees are good. In 1996 and 1997 when we were battling each other it was a great environment, and you could really feel the energy.

"Playing there took on greater significance and meaning because you thought about all of the history and all of the incredible moments that took place on that field. Standing on the same field as Babe Ruth, Lou Gehrig, Joe DiMaggio, and Mickey Mantle can be pretty humbling.

"I made sure I visited the monuments on a few occasions. It is a great place, and when you have a history like the Yankees, it makes it extra special. I remember in 1995 and again at the end of my career, a few photographers asked me to go out there and take photographs in front of Lou Gehrig's monument, and that was fun.

"The fans have always treated me really well at Yankee Stadium, and we all know that they can be tough. Truth is that they are very smart baseball fans and they react favorably to players who play hard regardless of their uniform—unless it's a Boston uniform, I guess. When you're not playing well, they will let you know it, but I always had great experiences at Yankee Stadium.

"Playing there after 9/11 was very powerful and very difficult. I met many of the children of police officers and firefighters who lost their lives on September 11. A lot of the kids were my children's age, and that made it especially poignant.

"I remember when the plans were in place to build Camden Yards. I just didn't think it made sense. We had all of this great Orioles history at Memorial Stadium, and I loved playing there. But when we played our first game at Camden Yards, that changed everything. It is such a beautiful place and such a great environment for baseball that I realized that sometimes change is good, and I knew that we could create a whole new set of memories and experiences in Oriole Park. Memorial Stadium will never be forgotten. This is a just a new place that is more comfortable

**OFF THE WALL**

**Yankee Stadium was owned by Rice University from 1962 until 1971, when the City of New York acquired the property through eminent domain for $2.5 million. Rice alumnus John Cox had acquired all the stadium's stock in 1955 and donated it all to his alma mater in 1962. The Knights of Columbus owned the land beneath the stadium, while Rice owned the ballpark itself.**

and a better environment to watch a game and better for the fans and the players. The memories of Memorial Stadium will last forever, and I guess that is how I hope the Yankees and their fans look at their new ballpark."

## CURT SCHILLING

The sight of blood oozing through the sock covering Schilling's right ankle remains an indelible image to baseball fans watching Game 6 of the American League Championship Series between the Red Sox and Yankees at the stadium on October 19, 2004. The bleeding resulted from sutures doctors inserted to hold together the Boston pitcher's torn tendon sheath. The instability of Schilling's ankle led to a rough outing in Game 1 against the Yankees, and many believed the right-hander was done for the Series. But thanks to the experimental medical procedure and sheer grit, Schilling came back to pitch seven strong innings and beat the Yankees to force a seventh game. The Red Sox won that contest, too, becoming the first team in baseball history to come back from a three-games-to-none deficit to win a series. Spurred on by Schilling's heroic performance, the Sox went on to sweep the St. Louis Cardinals for their first World Series title in 86 years.

"I could tell in the bullpen before Game 6 that the ankle would hold up. The tendon was not popping back and forth over the ankle bone. In Game 1, it had popped when I hit the

*Curt Schilling of the Boston Red Sox looks at his wounded ankle during Game 6 of the American League Championship on October 19, 2004, at Yankee Stadium. By the time the game was just a few innings old, blood was visibly seeping through Schilling's sock.*

top step of the dugout heading to the bullpen, and then pretty much every time I threw a ball or ran on it after that.

"I don't remember when I first noticed that blood was oozing through my sock. I think somewhere after the warm-up, when I was heading back into the dugout, is when it started. I didn't realize it was bleeding more than a little until sometime later. My foot was half numb, but there was enough blood running on the bottom of my foot that it was slipping inside the shoe, and I kept having to press my foot down to make sure my shoe was on right.

"The medical staff had done a great job with pain management. What happened that day was the Lord giving me the strength to put it all on him and just go out and compete. I was as stress-free as I had ever been once I knew the sutures would hold up.

"Some called it one of those unforgettable moments at Yankee Stadium, but I'm not sure I looked at it like that. I just realized that it happened within the confines of a Yankees–Red Sox game in October. It was a do-or-die game, and we won, and I helped. That was enough for me.

"We were so totally focused on the game at hand that I still believe we won that Series because we were able to play one inning, one out, and one game at a time from Game 4 on.

"Yankee Stadium definitely is one of my favorite places to pitch. The electricity in that stadium is unmatched when you go there as a Red Sox player.

"I became a Lou Gehrig fan once my wife, Shonda, and I got involved with ALS. I started to research who he really was and his story. The more I got to know him, the more impressed I became with his achievements in life and his impact on the game. I've only been out to his monument a few times. I took my oldest son, Gehrig, there when he was old enough to make the trip."

## PAUL MOLITOR

Molitor ripped 3,319 hits, drove in 1,307 runs, and stole 504 bases during his Hall of Fame career. He began and spent the majority of his career with the Milwaukee Brewers, but his high point came in 1993 with the Toronto Blue Jays, when he won World Series Most Valuable Player honors. He finished his career with the Minnesota Twins.

"My first road trip as a rookie was to Yankee Stadium. I remember arriving there early so I could walk through Monument Park. I had watched several games on television, but actually being there was very inspiring. To think you were going to play in the same place that Ruth, DiMaggio, and Mantle had played was kind of an out-of-body experience.

"Despite the jitters, I had a memorable first game there. The score was tied going into the ninth inning, and I was leading off. Sparky Lyle, the Yankees' ace reliever, had just come into the game, and as I was walking toward the batter's box, Graig Nettles walked over from third base to talk to Lyle. They were standing there talking and pointing at me. I didn't know what it was about, but it looked strange. The first pitch Lyle threw to me was a slider that hung, and I drove it into the left-field bleachers. As I was trotting around the bases, Nettles went back to talk to Lyle. After the game, I found out what they were talking about. Before I got into the box, Nettles told Lyle 'to look out because this guy likes to bunt.' And after I hit that home run, Lyle told him, 'That's the longest f*cking bunt I ever saw,' and Nettles responded, 'Well, you have to throw him more than one f*cking pitch.' I got a big kick out of that when some reporters relayed that conversation to me.

"In 1981 I experienced October baseball at Yankee Stadium for the first time. We beat the Yankees the first two games in Milwaukee, then headed to New York having to win just one of three to take the playoff series, but wound up getting swept. It certainly was an intimidating place for a young player, and the playoffs in the Bronx is a totally different atmosphere—incredibly intense.

"The fans there were more into the game than anyplace else we played. There always seemed to be big crowds there, and right from the start the fans were on you, trying to throw you off your game. Yankee Stadium was the first place I went to where the crowd would be clapping and up on its feet when their pitcher got two strikes on you. That all started with Ron Guidry during those great years he had in the late 1970s and early '80s.

"All the history and success the Yankees have had through the years added to the ballpark's mystique. One of the things I liked best was Bob Sheppard's voice. My name never sounded better at a ballpark than it did when Sheppard was saying it over the PA at the stadium.

"The fans were intimidating, but they also were fun. They were so vocal and so clever. Over time, you learn to kind of enjoy the interaction with them while you're in the on-deck circle. You'll never get them on your side, but you can earn their respect. If they sense that they can get inside somebody's head, it only gets worse. You definitely don't want to show them you are vulnerable or thin-skinned, or they'll kill you. I think, over time, they saw how I played hard and laughed at their good lines, and I earned their respect. I loved playing there. There definitely was no other place in baseball like it."

## JIM KAAT

To the current generation of Yankee fans, Kaat is known as one of the game's most astute broadcasters. But before announcing Bronx Bomber games for 13 seasons, Kaat was one of the most durable pitchers in baseball history. During his 25-year career—only Nolan Ryan and Tommy John played longer—Kaat won 283 games while pitching for five different clubs, including the Yankees in 1979 and '80. He won a record 16 Gold Gloves for fielding excellence at his position and was named to three All-Star teams. He retired from the Yankees' announcing team in September 2006.

"During my first trip to Yankee Stadium with the old Washington Senators, I couldn't help but notice how everyone kind of stopped what they were doing when Mickey Mantle stepped into the batting cage. Even opposing players would stop playing catch. You couldn't help but be in awe of Mickey in those days—the late 1950s, early '60s—because he was light-years in

*Minnesota Twin Jim Kaat, on the way to a shutout, pitches to Thurman Munson of the New York Yankees at Yankee Stadium on July 18, 1973.*

front of everybody as far as the way the ball sounded coming off his bat and how much power he had. I'll tell you, it was pretty intimidating for a young pitcher. You didn't want to spend too much time watching him take BP because it wasn't exactly a confidence booster. You were better off staying in the clubhouse where you couldn't see or hear the balls he was clobbering."

# JOHNNY PODRES

The Brooklyn Dodgers' 23-year-old southpaw battled injuries and bad luck during the 1955 season and wound up losing eight of his last 10 decisions to finish with a mediocre 9–10 record. But there was something about Podres that Brooklyn manager Walter Alston really liked, and he wound up handing him the ball for arguably the two most significant games in Brooklyn baseball history. Mixing a sneaky fastball with a wicked curve and a nasty change-up, Podres beat the Yankees in Game 3 of the '55 World Series and then blanked them 2–0 in Game 7 at Yankee Stadium to give Brooklyn its first and only Fall Classic title. "Next year" had finally arrived for the borough's long-suffering baseball fans, and a celebration ensued that even surpassed the one that followed the end of World War II.

"People in Brooklyn were dancing in the streets and drivers everywhere were honking their horns. Those people had waited a lifetime for this. And for it to come at the expense of the Yankees made it all the sweeter. It was the same feeling that Red Sox fans experienced in Boston in 2004. We had finally gotten that monkey off Brooklyn's back.

"I'll never forget a headline in one of the papers that day. In big, bold type, it read: 'WHO'S A BUM?'

"We had dropped the first two games of that Series, and no team had ever come back from a 2–0 deficit. Some of the sportswriters began predicting a Yankees sweep, especially when they found out that Alston was giving me the ball for Game 3. They were remembering how I pitched down the stretch, and they were thinking I was too young.

"I actually turned 23 on September 30, 1955—the date of Game 3. I threw a complete-game seven-hitter at Ebbets Field. That was a nice birthday present. After the game, Alston pulled me aside and told me I would be starting if there were a Game 7.

"We won the next two games, but the Yankees came back to beat us in Game 6 at the stadium. Whitey Ford was brilliant that day. I think he threw a four-hitter to beat us and even the Series.

"To this day, whenever I run into Whitey, I make sure I thank him, because if he didn't win that game, nobody would have remembered me.

"And they wouldn't have remembered Sandy Amoros, either. When we took the field for the bottom of the sixth, Alston switched Junior Gilliam from left to second base [in place of Don Zimmer, for whom he had pinch-hit in the top of the inning] and sent Sandy out to play left field.

"Billy Martin drew a leadoff walk and Gil McDougald followed with a bunt single. Yogi [Berra] was coming to the plate, and I was a little nervous because I knew he was a great clutch hitter and a great bad-ball hitter. Our outfield shifted around to the right because Yogi was left-handed and a pull hitter. But being

> **OFF THE WALL**
> The 2008 Major League Baseball All-Star Game will mark the fourth time the stadium has played host to the Midsummer Classic. It also was played there in 1939, 1960, and 1977.

Yogi, he crossed us up by looping an opposite-field drive toward the left-field corner.

"If Junior had been out there, I don't know if he would have been able to reach it because he was right-handed and he would have had to backhand it on the run. Fortunately, Sandy was left-handed, so he could catch it in front of him.

"I got myself in a little trouble again in the eighth when two runners reached, but I got out of it, and the ninth inning went smoothly. Once Pee Wee threw out Elston Howard, the celebration began.

"Not a day goes by when I don't run into someone who thanks me or wants to reminisce about it. I never tire talking about it. It was a once-in-a-lifetime experience."

## DENNIS ECKERSLEY

The Eck began his career as a starting pitcher and proved to be a good one, winning 20 games in 1978 and 17 in '79 for the Boston Red Sox. But he didn't become great until he converted from starter to closer in the late 1980s. Eckersley went on to record 390 saves, including 51 for the Oakland A's in 1992, when he won the American League MVP and Cy Young Award. Eckersley was named to six All-Star teams and was voted into the Baseball Hall of Fame in 2004.

"'Dong! Dong! Dong! Dong!' I can still hear those damn chimes they play after you give up a home run there—and, believe me, I gave up my share of them at Yankee Stadium. I got my first taste of the stadium in the mid-'70s when I played with the Cleveland Indians. We had a bad team back then, so I got beat up pretty good. I didn't have much support. Then I got traded to the Red Sox in 1978, and I started having a little success there because we had some pretty good lineups back then. I wound up winning 20 that year, and I'm pretty sure I went 4–0 against the Yankees, which wasn't an easy thing to do when you're facing Munson and Reggie and Chambliss and Nettles.

"In 1979, I remember pitching a game there against Catfish Hunter. It was supposed to be this big pitching duel, and it wound up being Home Run Derby. I served up five home runs and Catfish gave up several, too. Fortunately, the first four I gave up were solo shots, but then I gave up a two-run blast that finally sent me to the showers. I was awful.

"My best start there came in late September of '78. We had just suffered through the Boston Massacre up at Fenway. They had pounded us into submission and our 14-game lead was completely gone by then. In fact the Yankees had gone up on us by something like two-and-a-half games, and we needed a win or else we were toast. I wound up going seven, and we won to stay alive. It was like a playoff atmosphere at the stadium that day. Their fans could smell the blood. They wanted to finish us off once and for all, but they couldn't. That was our biggest win of the year, and we wound up finishing in a tie at the end of the regular season to set up that Bucky-freaking-Dent playoff game.

"Yankee Stadium was not a place I looked forward to pitch in. The combination of the great lineups they used to throw at you and that short porch in right field was pretty intimidating. I never felt completely comfortable on the mound there. The backstop seemed like it was a mile away from home plate and that resulted in this optical illusion that it's farther than 60'6" from the mound to home plate. I know that wasn't the case. But home plate just seemed farther away from you than it did in other ballparks.

"The fans also were intimidating, especially when I came in there with the Red Sox. They absolutely hated you. It was different when I came in with the Indians. Of course, we were bad, so they didn't get into it quite as much because they probably figured the Yankees were going to kick our ass, which they usually did. And when I came in later with the A's, the Yankees had gotten bad, so the fans weren't really into it. But those times in the late 1970s, early '80s, when the rivalry with the Red Sox was at its peak, that place was really rocking. I swear there were times when you could feel the ground shaking."

## JOHN "BOOG" POWELL

The big left-handed-hitting slugger spent 17 seasons in the big leagues, clubbing 339 homers and driving in 1,187 runs along the way. Powell earned All-Star honors four times and was named American League Most Valuable Player for the Baltimore Orioles in 1970.

"I'll always have fond memories of Yankee Stadium because it was the place where I played my first big-league game, got my first big-league hit, and drove in my first big-league run. I had a great season for the Rochester Red Wings, the Orioles' Triple A affiliate, in 1961—had over 30 dingers, close to 100 RBIs, and batted way over .300—and Baltimore called me up in September. I showed up at the stadium at about 3:00 in the afternoon, pulled on a big-league uniform for the first time, and headed out for batting practice. I'll never forget reaching the dugout and looking up at the three decks. I swear my jaw dropped. I'd never seen a ballpark that big. I gazed at the upper deck in right where I'd heard Ruth and Mantle had deposited some home runs, and I did a double take. I just couldn't believe anybody could hit a baseball that far.

> **OFF THE WALL**
>
> **The New York Black Yankees of the old Negro Leagues called Yankee Stadium home from 1936 to 1948.**

"My first time in the batter's box, I was so nervous my knees were knocking. I couldn't stop from thinking that this was the same batter's box that Ruth and Gehrig and Mickey had used. You could have rolled the ball up there and I would have swung at it, I was so in awe. I think I struck out on three straight pitches.

"But late in the game, I got a base hit and drove in a run, which wound up being the difference in the game. As you can imagine, I was pretty excited when I reached first base. I remember Moose Skowron, the Yankees' first baseman, coming over to me and asking me if that was my first hit. I was wearing this big smile, and I said, 'It sure is.' And he said in this gruff voice, 'Big deal.' Moose and I laughed about that moment in the seasons that followed, especially when my Orioles started to get the better of his teams.

"Being a left-handed power hitter made that short porch in right field pretty inviting. Of course, when I started to have some success in the big leagues, the scouting reports called for the Yankees pitchers to pitch me outside, so over time I hit my share of 430-, 440-foot fly-outs to Death Valley in left-center. That was pretty frustrating. I'd go with the pitch and hit the crap out of it, and there's Mickey standing out there, catching it in his back pocket. Those were home runs in any other park, but not Yankee Stadium.

"There was one time, though, when I got one over Mickey's head and it bounced around those monuments they used to have in the field of play in center. I was a big guy who didn't run real well, so I turned what would have been an inside-the-park homer for most guys into a double. A stand-up double, I might add."

## JOHNNY ANTONELLI

One of baseball's original "bonus babies," Antonelli was signed by the Boston Braves out of high school, but his career didn't take off until he was traded to the New York Giants before the 1954 season in exchange for Bobby Thomson. The 6'1" left-hander wound up going 21–7 with a National League–leading 2.30 earned-run average. Antonelli saved his best for last that season, picking up a win and a save in the World Series as the Giants swept the Cleveland Indians. Antonelli made the NL All-Star team five times, led the league in shutouts twice, and compiled a 126–110 won-lost record. He finished his career in 1961, pitching briefly for the Indians.

"We went into New York for a three-game series and our manager, Jimmie Dykes, asked me if I could start a game, and I said, 'Sure.' I had been in the big leagues more than 10 seasons, but they all had been in the National League, so this was my first time in Yankee Stadium, and it was naturally quite a thrill.

"I actually had the Yankees beat that day. We were up 3–1 going into the bottom of the eighth, and they loaded the bases. There were two outs and Mickey was coming to the plate. Dykes visited the mound and asked me what I wanted to do. I was thinking to myself, 'What a crazy question.' I had nowhere to put him, and Moose Skowron was on deck, and he was on a pace to hit 30 homers that season. So it was a case of 'pick your poison.'

"I decided to pitch to Mickey, and I got two strikes on him. I figured I'd waste one and see if I could get him to go fishing. Well, I threw a pitch about a foot outside, and he one-armed it to right-center field for a bases-clearing triple to put the Yankees up by a run. Skowron came up, and I got him to pop out on the first pitch to end the inning. In hindsight, maybe I should have walked [Mantle] with the bases loaded and pitched to Skowron.

But I never expected anybody to be able to hit a waste-pitch like that. It showed just how strong he was, to be able to hit a bad ball, one-handed, that far."

## BROOKS ROBINSON

Known as the "Human Vacuum Cleaner," Robinson won a record 16 consecutive Gold Gloves at third base for the Baltimore Orioles during his 23-year big-league career. His glove work during the 1970 World Series against the Cincinnati Reds won him Most Valuable Player honors and the Hickok Belt as the top professional athlete in America. Robinson finished his career with 268 homers, 2,848 hits, and a .267 batting average. He was inducted into the Baseball Hall of Fame in 1983.

"People may not know this, but I had a chance to sign with the Yankees. But Baltimore came after me and offered me a major league bonus. Back in the 1950s, if a team gave you a bonus of more than $4,000, they had to keep you on the big-league roster. The Orioles weren't very good back then, so it looked like a better opportunity for me to play big-league ball earlier.

"I'm glad I had the opportunity to play at Yankee Stadium a couple hundred times in my career because it's the place where Babe Ruth hit all those home runs and Lou Gehrig delivered his famous speech. History-wise, no stadium can ever match it.

"But I'm also glad I only had to visit there a few times a season. It would have been brutal to play 81 home games there every season because I was a right-handed batter, and that place was torture because the fences were so far away. I remember seeing that film clip of Joe DiMaggio hitting that deep drive in the World Series and Al Gionfriddo making that wonderful catch against the bullpen fence, and Joe kicking the dirt in disgust. There were several times I hit some long balls there that should have been homers, and I wanted to kick something.

"There was one game, though, where I hit two home runs at Yankee Stadium. One I pulled straight down the left-field line, and the other I poked straight down the right-field line. Probably the two shortest home runs I ever hit, but they kind of made up for those 400-foot outs I hit there.

"I always said that teams that came in there to play were at a disadvantage because it usually took an hour to two hours to get to the ballpark from your downtown hotel, and then when you got off the bus, there would be fans there screaming at you, saying, 'Youse guys are going to get it,' and most of the time, they were right because the Yankees usually had the better teams."

## DOM DIMAGGIO

He was overshadowed, as most every player of that era was, by his big brother, Joe DiMaggio. And that's too bad because Dom DiMaggio put together a big-league career that would be the envy of most. Known as "the Little Professor" because he stood only 5'9" and wore glasses, Dom made the American League

*Dom DiMaggio (left), pictured here with his brother, Joe, at Yankee Stadium on Old-Timers' Day in 1965. Though Dom never received the recognition his Yankee brother did, he was a formidable baseball player in his own right.*

All-Star team seven times and batted .298 during his career with the Boston Red Sox. A superb center fielder, some believed that he was actually a better defensive player than his brother, Joe.

"I liked playing in Yankee Stadium because I had plenty of room to roam. The only thing that bothered me was the monuments being in play. There was one game we had against the Yankees where I caught two balls on the run about six feet from the monuments. You certainly didn't want to bang into those things because they were made of granite and they weren't going to give any ground.

"I know Joe didn't always like hitting there because it was so dang far in the left-center-field power alleys. He hit an awful lot of balls in his career that would have been home runs in any other park.

"I remember late in the season one year, Joe was battling for the RBI title, and he came up late in the game with the bases loaded and hit a shot to left-center against us. I ran and I ran and I ran and I ran and I wound up just barely catching the ball in the webbing of my glove. I hated to do that to my brother, but we all were battling for our paychecks in those days, and I didn't want anybody accusing me of showing favoritism to my brother. That night we were eating dinner together at a restaurant in New York, and I told him that if that ball had been about two inches higher I never would have gotten it, and he would have had at least a triple and three RBIs. He didn't seem too pleased with me. He just said, 'I wish it had been a few inches higher.' That was Joe. He was such a competitor.

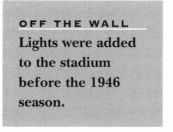

**OFF THE WALL**

**Lights were added to the stadium before the 1946 season.**

"They had a Joe DiMaggio Day at the stadium on the same day we were in town to play the Yankees, so they had me standing out there with Joe near home plate. They had flown my mom and dad in from San Francisco, and when they escorted them down from the stands, my mom walked right past Joe and gave me a big hug. The crowd roared because they thought she was jokingly snubbing Joe. The truth is that Joe had had dinner with them the night before, so he had seen Mom already. We had just come into New York that day, so I hadn't seen Mom yet. Like I said, the crowd got a big kick out of that. Here it is Joe DiMaggio Day, and I'm the one getting the first hug."

## BOBBY GRICH

During his big-league career with the Baltimore Orioles and California Angels, Grich earned American League All-Star honors six times and won four Gold Gloves for his fielding prowess. Grich led the league in home runs in 1981 and finished his career with 224 homers, 864 RBIs, and a .266 batting average.

"I went there for the first time with the Orioles in 1970, and when we crossed over the East River and saw that massive building, I got goose bumps. When you walk onto that field, you know you are someplace really special. You really can feel the ghosts of the Babe and Lou Gehrig there. I'm a golf fanatic, and the only other time in my life when I felt like that was when I played Augusta National for the first time. As you walk that course, you think about the great shots that guys like Jack Nicklaus and Gene Sarazen made at certain holes. It's the same way at the stadium. You think about where Ruth and Mantle hit balls into the upper deck. And where Gehrig stood for his famous speech.

"It will always be special to me personally because it's where I hit my first big-league home run. I remember it like it was yesterday. It was a 2–1 slider from Stan Bahnsen, and I pulled it right down the left-field line. It's a good thing I pulled it, because back in those days, that fence jutted out real quickly. A few more feet to the right, and it would have been a harmless fly-out."

---

**OFF THE WALL**

## YANKEE BALLPARKS

The new Yankee Stadium will be the sixth ballpark the team has called home. Twice during the Yankees' history, they've shared parks with National League clubs—the New York Giants for eight seasons early in the 20th century and the New York Mets in the mid-1970s while Yankee Stadium was undergoing a nearly $200 million renovation. Here are the Yankees' "home" diamonds since their inception as the Highlanders in 1903.

| 1903–1912 | Hilltop Park | Manhattan |
|-----------|--------------|-----------|
| 1913–1922 | Polo Grounds | Manhattan |
| 1923–1973 | Yankee Stadium | Bronx |
| 1974–1975 | Shea Stadium | Queens |
| 1976–2008 | Yankee Stadium | Bronx |

6

# ATHLETES FROM OTHER SPORTS REMINISCE

## FRANK GIFFORD

He is best known as the longtime play-by-play voice of ABC's *Monday Night Football* telecasts, but long before Gifford became a sports broadcasting icon, he was a superb football player. An All-American running back at the University of Southern California, Gifford was selected in the first round of the 1952 draft by the New York Giants. In 12 seasons in New York, Gifford earned seven Pro Bowl invitations and was named the NFL's Most Valuable Player in 1956 after leading the Giants to the championship in their first season at Yankee Stadium. He accounted for 91 touchdowns during his career—34 rushing, 43 receiving, and 14 passing—and was elected to the Pro Football Hall of Fame in 1977. Gifford had many magical moments at the stadium—and one harrowing one, too. During a 1960 home game against Philadelphia, Eagles linebacker Chuck Bednarik blindsided Gifford on a pass play. The Giants star suffered a concussion and had to be removed from the field on a stretcher. He took a year off to pursue his broadcasting career, but missed playing the game so much that he returned to the Giants in 1962, and a year later, wound up making the Pro Bowl at his third different position—flanker.

"We had spent my first few seasons playing in the old Polo Grounds across the river from Yankee Stadium, and the place was—to be kind—a dump. So when we heard that we would be playing our home games in the stadium in 1956 we were ecstatic. The first thing we did when we got into the stadium that fall was walk around the Yankees clubhouse and see whose locker we got. [Linebacker] Sam Huff said he shared Mickey Mantle's locker, but I swear he's mistaken. I'm positive I had Mantle's locker. I guess we'll never really know.

"I had been in New York for four years to that point, and I had spent a lot of time at Toots Shor's, the old watering hole of New York athletes, writers, actors, and comedians, so I had gotten to know some of the Yankees. To know that we were going to be sharing the stadium with them made it more special.

"I still say that the Giants' move to Yankee Stadium was one of the things that helped put pro football on the map. Up until that time, the NFL was really on the back burner; we were second-class citizens. Hell, it was such an afterthought in those days that you didn't have sportswriters assigned regularly to the Giants the way they were for three baseball teams in town. Even though the Polo Grounds was in New York, we might as well have been playing in the North Pole as far as newspaper coverage was concerned. But when we won that championship in our first year at Yankee Stadium, the media and the fans really started to take notice. Yankee Stadium helped legitimize the NFL in the largest media market in the United States.

"Of course, the '58 championship game was the one that everyone points to as the NFL's launching pad. I think Johnny Unitas became Johnny Unitas that day. That game really cemented his legacy. And Raymond Berry had a huge day that sometimes gets overlooked because everyone focused on Unitas.

"I'm, of course, biased, but the thing I remember most is the third-down running play late in regulation. We were leading by three points with just over two minutes to go, and if we got the first down, we could have run the clock out, and people wouldn't still be talking about that game 50 years later.

**OFF THE WALL**
**The "Dee-FENSE!" chant, now commonplace at most football games, traces its origins to New York Giants home games at Yankee Stadium.**

It was a power play, off tackle, and I thought I made the first down, but the referee disagreed. There was a big pileup on the play, and the Colts' big defensive tackle, Gino Marchetti, wound up breaking his leg. Gino was at the bottom of the pile and screaming for guys to get off of him, and the referee was so intent on unpiling the mass of humanity that he wasn't worrying about the spot.

"That set up fourth down, and some more second-guessing. I really don't know if we made the right call deciding to punt instead of going for it. We were a very tired football team at that point—more tired and beat up than the Colts because we'd had to play the week before just to get into the championship game, while Baltimore had the week off. Our head coach, Jim Lee Howell, didn't bother consulting our offensive coordinator, Vince Lombardi, or our defensive coordinator, Tom Landry. He just sent in the punt team.

"Don Chandler got off a great punt, and we had the Colts pinned back at their 14 with two minutes to go. It looked like there was no way Baltimore was going to be able to drive that far against our top-ranked defense to tie it. But, like I said, our defense was so fatigued that our star pass rushers, Jim Katcavage and Andy Robustelli, looked as if they were running in sand. They were whipped. And that's not a good situation, especially when you were going against Johnny U. He just picked us apart. I kept waiting for us to pick him off, but it never happened. So, they tied it, then won it in OT, and though the final score wasn't to our liking, we had added a chapter to the history books of the NFL and Yankee Stadium.

"I played in all the great stadiums, but nothing compared to Yankee Stadium. It was just such a classy, historical place. There was something almost haunting about walking the same hallways and playing on the same field that Ruth and Gehrig had. I think the voice of public address announcer Bob Sheppard added to the specialness. He's such a regal man. It still sends chills up my spine listening to him say my name.

*Frank Gifford, of the New York Giants, is carried from the field on a stretcher after receiving a brutal hit from Chuck Bednarik at Yankee Stadium on November 20, 1960.*

"The Bednarik hit has gotten a lot of play through the years, and I really believe it was blown out of proportion. It looked a lot worse than it was. He drilled me in the chest and the ground was semifrozen, and my head kind of whiplashed against the dirt. If we had CAT scans back then, I probably would have been cleared to play in a few weeks.

"I definitely was a little hazy when I was in the locker room. I recall hearing somebody say, 'He's dead.' Well, I knew I wasn't dead because I was talking to our medical people. They were referring to a stadium security guard who had suffered a heart attack. I learned afterward that there were a lot of rumors flying that I had died from the hit. I can only imagine what people were thinking when the deceased security guard was taken out of the stadium with a white sheet covering his face. A lot has been written about that hit forcing me out of the game for a year. But the truth is, I was doing both television and radio broadcasting in New York at the time, and I figured it was time to pursue that career year-round. Well, that first season away from the game, in 1961, I really missed playing. I'd go work out sometimes with the Giants' scout team, and I would be beating guys on pass routes. One night driving home, I said to myself, 'The broadcasting career will be there for many years, but you only have a limited window to be an athlete.' So I decided to make a comeback, and I'm glad I did.

"1962 wound up being a great season for us, especially offensively. Y.A. Tittle was our quarterback, and there was a game at the stadium against the Washington Redskins when he threw seven touchdown passes to tie the NFL record for most TD passes in a game. That was one of those magical games when everything we tried worked. We couldn't be stopped. I remember telling Y.A. that we better stop scoring because we had to play these guys again later in the season, and he laughed. He actually didn't want to go back into the game to go for that seventh touchdown pass because he didn't want to rub it in. But the coaches made him. That season we led the NFL in scoring, and we thought we had a great chance to win the championship. We played the Green Bay Packers at home for the title, and we totally lost the home-field advantage because the weather was more like what you would expect in Green Bay. It was nine degrees at game time, and the winds were blowing 20 to 30 miles per hour. We couldn't get anything going with the passing game, and Green Bay beat us 16–7.

"I'll never forgot the feeling I had walking off the field at Yankee Stadium a final time in 1964. The team had gotten old all at once, and we had a really bad season. Both Y.A. and I were retiring, and I remember us standing at the foot of the dugout after that last game

**OFF THE WALL**
**National Hockey League executives inquired about using the field for an outdoor regular-season game between the New York Rangers and New York Islanders on New Year's Day, but arrangements couldn't be worked out, and the venue was switched to Ralph Wilson Stadium in Orchard Park, New York, with the Buffalo Sabres serving as the host team.**

and looking out at the field and saying, 'Good-bye, Yankee Stadium.' It was a pretty sad moment for both of us."

## CARMEN BASILIO

While picking onions on the family farm as a boy growing up in upstate New York, Carmen Basilio would often daydream. A huge fan of heavyweight champion Joe Louis and the New York Yankees, Basilio fantasized about what it would feel like to box for a title in front of a huge crowd at the stadium. On September 23, 1957, he found out, winning a punishing, 15-round split decision against the legendary Sugar Ray Robinson in front of 38,072 fans to become the middleweight champion of the world. The battle between the tall, stylish Robinson and the short, iron-jawed Basilio was named the fight of the year by *Ring* magazine and earned the Canastota Clouter his biggest boxing payday ($211,629) and the 1957 Hickok Belt as the top professional athlete in America. To many boxing fans, Basilio, who finished his ring career with a 56–16–7 record, was a real-life Rocky Balboa.

"Of all my fights—and I had some pretty good ones in my day—that one was the most special because it fulfilled a lifelong dream of mine. And the check I received for that one didn't hurt, either. When I was young, my father and I would listen to Joe Louis fights on the radio, and that's what planted the seed in my head about becoming a boxer. People told me I was foolish to want to become a boxer because it was a brutal occupation, but I didn't want to spend the rest of my life picking onions in the hot summer heat. To me, that was more brutal than boxing.

"Yankee Stadium was the capital of boxing back then. It became a place where a lot of the really big matches were fought

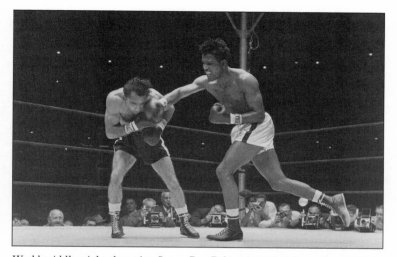

*World middleweight champion Sugar Ray Robinson (right) fires a long right to the face of challenger and welterweight champion Carmen Basilio during the second round of their 15-round middleweight title fight at Yankee Stadium on September 23, 1957.* Photo courtesy of AP/Wide World Images.

back in the '20, '30s, '40s, and '50s. Guys like Jack Dempsey and Joe Louis and Rocky Marciano and Sugar Ray fought there. Plus, being a fan of Yankees like Joe DiMaggio and Yogi Berra made fighting there special for me, too.

"But there's one other reason why that win was so important to me. It helped me settle a grudge and pay Sugar Ray back for snubbing me the way he did when I was just an up-and-comer. I remember standing outside the Statler Hotel in Times Square with my wife in 1952 when Robinson and his crew pulled up in this big, pink Cadillac. I was a boxing nobody at the time, and Sugar Ray was king. I told my wife, 'I'm going to introduce myself to him.' I said, 'Mr. Robinson, my name is Carmen Basilio, I just fought my second television fight.' Before I could get another word out, he just blew by me. He made me feel like I was dirt beneath his feet. I was really pissed. I went back to my wife and said, 'One of these days I'm going to fight that son of a bitch, and I'm going to kick his ass.'

"I wouldn't say I kicked his ass, but I did beat him up pretty good. My corner was worried that he was going to be awarded the victory because he was the champ and they say you have to knock out the champ in order to take the title away from him. They told me not to celebrate after the 15th round ended. But I wasn't worried. I knew I had convinced the judges that I controlled more of the fight than he did.

"One other thing made that night memorable: I got to dress in Casey Stengel's office for the fight. Through the years, I got to know Yogi Berra and Whitey Ford and Mickey Mantle, and some of the Yankees would come to my fights in the offseason. New York was a great sports town and a great boxing town back then.

> **OFF THE WALL**
> **Three NFL championship games were played at Yankee Stadium, with the Giants beating the Chicago Bears in 1956 and losing to the Baltimore Colts in 1958 and to the Green Bay Packers in 1962.**

The people there always supported me well. I think they liked the fact that I was Italian and that I came from the working class and wasn't afraid to take a punch in order to land one. I think more people in that crowd at Yankee Stadium that night could relate to me than they could to a natural athlete like Sugar Ray. I was the underdog, and I was a guy who kept his mouth shut and let my fists do my talking. Sugar Ray was a great fighter, but he was arrogant, and that turned a lot of people off. I know it turned me off. But I was able to make him eat his words. He knew who the hell I was after that fight."

## ART DONOVAN

A Bronx native, Donovan grew up a 15¢ subway ride from Yankee Stadium. He remembers seeing Lou Gehrig and Joe DiMaggio play on several occasions and vividly recalls that late August day in 1948 when Babe Ruth's funeral procession drove through his neighborhood on its way to the cemetery. Art's dad, Art Donovan Sr., was regarded as the greatest boxing official of all time and worked several championship bouts, including the 1936 heavyweight championship between Joe Louis and Max Schmeling, at the famous ballpark. But Junior's biggest stadium thrill would come in 1958 when he played defensive tackle for the Baltimore Colts against the Giants in "the greatest football game ever played." A member of the Pro Football Hall of Fame, Donovan would gain wider acclaim in the late 1980s as a wisecracking guest on *Late Night with David Letterman.* Viewers fell in love with the jovial Donovan, whose humorous stories of his old football days usually had people in stitches. In 1987, Donovan collaborated on *Fatso,* an autobiography that made the *New York Times* best-seller list.

"We played the Giants during the regular season in 1958, and they beat us by three points. We didn't have John Unitas that day, so that explains a lot. I remember, as they were running out the clock, they were mocking us and laughing at us. That ticked me off. I called 'em a bunch of rat bastards and picked up some dirt and threw it at 'em. I told them we were going to play them again in the championship game, and we'd make them eat their words.

"The day before the championship game, we walked down from the Grand Concourse Plaza Hotel to the stadium to practice, and people kept telling us, 'The Giants are going to kill you tomorrow.' And we hollered back that we were going to shove the football up the Giants' ass. They laughed, and we laughed, and later when got back to the hotel, we ran into many of those same people and had coffee with them and joked back and forth. I think they appreciated the fact that I was a Bronx boy. But I had to remind them that sentimentality would be out the window the next day because the Giants didn't sign my paycheck.

"We jumped out to a 14–0 lead, and I was feeling pretty good. But we managed to piss it away, and with two minutes left in the game we were down three points and pinned back at our 14-yard line. I remember turning to Gino Marchetti on the sideline and saying, 'If we lose this freaking game, it will be an absolute travesty because we are definitely the better football team.'

"Fortunately, we had Unitas in this game, and he dissected their defense. He got us into position for the tying points and the field-goal unit trotted onto the field. I was part of that unit because I was a fatass, and they put all the fatasses out there to form a wall so the defense couldn't block the kick. I remember lining up for the kick and seeing several Giants lining up right over me. I'm yelling to Jim Parker, next to me, to give me some help, and he said, 'Help yourself, I've got two guys over me, too.' We snapped the ball, and I got knocked on my ass, but fortunately the kick was good. If you look at a picture of that tying field goal, you'll see No. 70 of the Colts sitting on his keister. That's me.

> **OFF THE WALL**
> **The New York Cosmos of the North American Soccer League played home games at Yankee Stadium in 1971 and 1976. The '76 Cosmos featured Pelé, the Brazilian star who is regarded by many as the greatest soccer player of all time.**

"The Giants supposedly not only had the better players but the better coaches. They had Vince Lombardi and Tom Landry and Jim Lee Howell on that staff. But we had a pretty good coach, too. In fact, I believe Weeb Ewbank is the best coach in the history of the NFL. Hell, he took two bad football teams—us and the Jets—and wound up winning championships with them. He wasn't always a lot of fun to play for, but that little weasel sure knew his football.

"To win that game just a few blocks down from where I lived was a dream come true. It was beyond my wildest imagination. After the game, I stayed in New York and went to the apartment where I grew up for a party. Most of my relatives were Giants fans, so they were pretty down at first. But after a few beers they were celebrating the fact that the hometown boy had won a championship. I wish I had a dollar for every person who told me they were at that game. It's like Marchetti told me: 'There were 72,000 people at that game, and I've already met a million of them.'

## SAM HUFF

The New York Giants selected Sam Huff out of West Virginia University in the third round of the 1956 National Football League draft, but his pro career nearly ended before it began. Giants head coach Jim Lee Howell didn't know where to play Huff, and the rookie became so disillusioned that he was ready to quit the team until assistant coach Vince Lombardi talked him out of it. An injury in the third game of the season opened a spot for Huff at middle linebacker, and he wound up occupying the position until he was traded to Washington following the 1963 season. Known as one of the most physical players in NFL history, Huff led the Giants to the 1956 championship and earned four Pro Bowl invitations. No. 70 remains one of the most popular Giants of all time. He was elected to the Pro Football Hall of Fame in Canton, Ohio, in 1982.

"All of us players on the Giants were well aware of the history of Yankee Stadium. You knew that this was the place where Babe Ruth and Joe DiMaggio and Mickey Mantle did great things, so we knew we had a lot to live up to when the stadium became our home, too, in 1956. This was the Home of Champions, and we wanted to hold up our end, and I think we did. In fact we won it all that first year. We put a licking on the Chicago Bears in the NFL championship game that December at the stadium. It was a licking the Yankees certainly would have been proud of.

> **OFF THE WALL**
> The stadium underwent its first major facelift in 1928 when the triple-deck grandstand in left field was extended beyond the foul pole to its current termination point. The right-field upper deck was extended beyond the foul pole in 1937.

"We actually got to know a lot of the Yankees because we shared the home-team locker room with them when our seasons overlapped in September and early October. I actually shared a locker with Mickey Mantle. He was a country boy from

Oklahoma, and I was a country boy from West Virginia, so we really hit it off. Great guy.

"I can't think of a better place to play football than the old stadium. The fans there were demanding, but that was okay with us. They expected you to give your best effort, and they let you know when you weren't. There was something about our defense that they really connected with. Our offense struggled a lot in the mid-to-late 1950s, and the fans booed them pretty good. It got so bad that they started introducing our defense instead of the offense before the game, and that was just fine with us.

"Today, you can go to just about any football game in the country and hear fans chanting 'Defense! Defense! Defense!' Well, the Giants fans at Yankee Stadium were the first to chant that. It still brings chills to my spine when I think back to how loud our fans were in that stadium.

"Of course, Yankee Stadium is the place where the greatest game in football history was staged. Unfortunately, we were on the losing end of it, but it's still great knowing that we were part of something that really helped launch the NFL to a popularity it hadn't known before. I don't remember a lot of particulars from that '58 championship game. All I know is that we threw everything we could at Johnny Unitas, and he was just about unstoppable down the stretch. I remember him leading the Colts down the field for the tying field goal at the end of regulation.

"We were dog-tired, and as we headed to the sideline after time expired, I just figured the game was over and we and the

Colts would be declared cochampions and we'd split the money down the middle. But then one of the referees came over to our coaches and said they needed our captains for the coin toss. I said, 'What for?' And they told me that we were going to play overtime. Now, it might sound like I had gotten hit in the head too many times by Jim Brown, but my response wasn't so dumb when you consider that there had never been an overtime game in the history of the NFL up to that point.

"The thing I remember about the overtime is that Unitas hadn't cooled off one bit. He kept finding Raymond Berry for first-down completions. Unitas-to-Berry, Unitas-to-Berry, Unitas-to-Berry. It was like a broken record. And that set up the winning touchdown on Alan Ameche's run. It was a really tough one to lose, especially in front of our fans.

"One of my greatest thrills at the stadium actually came after the Giants had traded me to the Washington Redskins in the mid-'60s. My first game back as an opposing player, our coaches had our defensive starters announced in the pregame. I didn't know how the fans would react. I thought there might be a chance they would shower me in boos. But when Bob Sheppard said my name over the PA in the special way only he can, there was a deafening ovation from the 70,000 fans. It was so loud and lasted so long that it drowned out the rest of the names Sheppard announced. Afterward, some of the New York reporters told me it was the loudest ovation they had heard at the stadium since the days of Babe Ruth."

## RAYMOND BERRY

Despite possessing average speed and below-average eyesight, Berry blossomed into one of the game's greatest wide receivers, earning a spot on the league's 75th anniversary team and a bust in the Pro Football Hall of Fame. He and Baltimore Colts quarterback Johnny Unitas developed into one of football's all-time most dangerous passing combinations. And they were never more in sync than during the 1958 NFL championship game against the New York Giants at Yankee Stadium when they hooked up 12 times for 178 yards and a touchdown. It wasn't until years after retiring from football that Berry realized the significance of that game on his career and the history of the NFL.

"I guess the thing I remember most was that final drive during regulation when I caught three passes on three consecutive plays to set up Steve Myhra's 20-yard field goal that sent the game into overtime. I spent probably four or five decades of my life in football as a player and a coach, and I can't recall a receiver getting his number called three consecutive plays during a two-minute drill. The year before John died, he and his wife visited us, and I finally asked him why he had taken the chance of going to the well that often, and he said, "I figured if I threw it to you, you would catch it." John had a great sense of humor, so I don't know if he was joking or not. But I'm sure glad I got open, and I'm sure glad I didn't drop any of those throws, because we needed all of them in order to come back and win.

*Alan Ameche (No. 35), of the Baltimore Colts, runs the ball during the NFL Championship Game on December 28, 1958, against the New York Giants at Yankee Stadium. Ameche scored for the Colts in overtime as they defeated the Giants 23–17. This was the first overtime game in NFL history.*

"I think part of our success on that drive and during the drive for the winning touchdown by Alan Ameche in overtime was a result of all the extra time John and I put in working together. He and I would often spend time before and after practices working together so that things would become second nature to us. And we talked an awful lot about scenarios, too. We'd talk about what we would do if the defense did this to me or that to me, and how we could adjust on the fly.

"I've also got to give our coach, Weeb Ewbank, a lot of credit. Before the game, he told John, 'We aren't going to be able to run the football against that Giants defense, so be ready to put the ball up a lot.' It actually turned out to be a great day to throw the ball. Even though it was late December, the weather in New York was in the 40s with no precipitation, so the field was in great shape, really good traction.

**OFF THE WALL**

**The Gotham Bowl was scheduled to be played at Yankee Stadium in 1960 but had to be canceled because no opponent could be found for Oregon State University. The 1961 game was moved to the Polo Grounds, while the 1962 game was played at the stadium. Nebraska defeated the University of Miami 36–34, but the bowl game was discontinued after that year because only 6,166 spectators were in attendance.**

"Weeb was smart enough to know that John had a great football mind and great instincts, so he left the play-calling to him. John was like an offensive coordinator out there on the field; he was amazing.

"The dramatic finish of that game clearly made it special, but so did the concentration of talent that was out there on that field. There were 13 players from that game who wound up in the Hall of Fame, and don't forget about the coaches. The Giants offensive coordinator was Vince Lombardi, and their defensive coordinator was Tom Landry. But I'd put Weeb up against either of those guys. To me, he was one of the three greatest coaches in the history of the game, and his performance that day was just another big feather in his cap.

"That final drive in regulation was an early-day version of the no-huddle offense. We'd complete a pass, line up and run a play again, then do it all over again. The Giants defense had no chance to adjust or substitute guys in. We had to operate like that because we had no timeouts left and we had to go about 70 yards in under two minutes. Again, all that extra work John and I put in really came into play in that situation.

"It was really strange when we did tie it up and it went into overtime because none of us had any experience with playing a fifth quarter of football. The Giants wound up winning the coin flip, and our defense held 'em and forced 'em to punt. When we came out onto the field, there was no doubt in our minds that we were going to go 80 yards and win this game. And our mind-set was to go down and score a touchdown, because Myhra had had a kick blocked earlier in the game, and even though he had kicked that field goal to send the game into overtime, we didn't want to take any chances. I wound up catching two balls for 33 yards on that drive, and Ameche capped it off by scoring from the 1.

"As I headed to our bus after showering, I remember seeing NFL commissioner Bert Bell out there on the sidewalk with tears in his eyes. It wasn't until several years later that I understood why he was crying. He understood long before any of us about the significance of this game. He was like a guy who had witnessed his first child being born. He realized this game was the start of big things for the NFL. To this day, I run into people who say they saw that game on television and that's what got them hooked on pro football. They, in turn, passed on that love for the NFL to their children and grandchildren, and that's why it's become so popular today.

"Another thing I didn't realize at the time was how appropriate it was that this game was played at Yankee Stadium. There's no sports arena in the country with more history, so it's kind of neat that the most historically significant pro football game wound up being played there. And it was extra special for me because, even though I grew up in Paris, Texas—the heart of football country—I grew up a huge Yankees fan."

# FANS REMINISCE

## LINDA RUTH TOSETTI

The granddaughter of the iconic Babe Ruth resides in Connecticut and has been a lifelong fan of the Boston Red Sox. When BoSox loyalists learn of her famous baseball lineage, they invariably ask her why she waited so long to get rid of the "Curse of the Bambino." Upon learning she is a Red Sox supporter, Yankee fans usually tell her that her grandfather must be spinning in his grave.

"I didn't go to Yankee Stadium for the first time until I was 20 years old, back around 1975. I went with my mom, who they had invited back for a ceremony they were having for my grandfather. My mom got to go on the field, and when they announced her as the daughter of Babe Ruth, the whole place erupted. The applause was deafening. That was the first time I had ever heard my grandfather's name announced in a ballpark, so it was quite a revelation for me. When my mom got back to her seat, all I could say to her was, 'Wow, Ma, I never heard anything like that.' And she turned to me and said, 'Linda, the Babe's name is still magic.'

"Even though I'm a diehard Red Sox fan, I still get a thrill going to Yankee Stadium. Every time I walk into the place, the hairs stand up on the back of my neck. It has a different feel to it than Fenway. I can feel the energy of my grandfather and all those great Yankees players who followed him.

**OFF THE WALL**

**In the 84-year history of the stadium, the Yankees have drawn roughly 151 million spectators.**

"I remember being back there in 1994 for a television interview some company wanted to do with me and Paul Hopkins, the old Washington Senators pitcher who gave up homer number 59 to my grandfather during his 60-homer season back in 1927. When the interviews ended, Paul asked me if I wanted to check out the Babe Ruth monument, and I said yes. We got out there, and the gate was locked. A security guard came over and asked us if he could help us out. I told him that there was a monument to my grandfather in there that we wanted to see. And he asked me who my grandfather was. When I told him 'Babe Ruth,' he shook his head and asked me why he should believe me. I pointed to my face, and he obviously could see my grandfather's likeness in me, so he let us in.

"We went and looked at my grandfather's monument, and that was really cool. The gates to center field happened to be open, and I looked at Paul, and Paul looked at me, and we said, 'Why not?' So we walked onto the field. We went to the mound. It was nearly 50 years since he had been back to the stadium, and as he stood on the rubber, he said, 'This place looks a lot bigger than I remember it being.'

"It obviously bothers me that they are ripping down The House That Ruth Built. But sometimes you can't fight change. They can call the new place 'The House That the Boss Built,' but I believe it still will be my grandfather's place because it will still be the home of the Yankees, and it was my granddad who got the ball rolling for them way back when. I think the spirits of the Babe and all those other great ballplayers the Yankees have had will walk across the street to the new place. You can rip down stadiums, but you can't destroy spirits."

## BILL POLIAN

As the architect of Super Bowl teams in Buffalo and Indianapolis and a five-time NFL Executive of the Year, Polian one day may be enshrined in the Pro Football Hall of Fame. But that wasn't his dream growing up just six subway stops north of Yankee Stadium. Polian's childhood dream wasn't to become an NFL general manager, but rather to play center field for the Yankees.

"I was six years old the first time my grandfather, Joseph McLaughlin, took me to a Yankees game. It was on the last weekend of the regular season, and the Yankees were playing the Red Sox in a pivotal series, and Joe DiMaggio hit a big home run. It wasn't until years later when I read David Halberstam's book, *1949*, that I realized just how big a series that was.

*Mickey Mantle was a Yankee powerhouse who was known for his ability to hit the ball farther than anybody else.*

"I was hooked from my first game, and from the seventh grade on, my buddies and I would go to about 75 games a summer between Yankee Stadium and the Polo Grounds. We usually sat in the bleachers. The tickets were 50¢. You couldn't beat the price.

"I remember Mickey Mantle almost from the time he was a rookie in 1951. I was there in 1963 when he hit the ball off the façade in right field. We were sitting in the left-field bleachers, so we had a great view of it. I thought for sure it was going out of the stadium. It was a typical Mantle blast. I saw him play regularly, and he would just hit the ball farther than anybody else.

"I also went to the famous Colts-Giants NFL championship game in '58 that went into overtime. We were able to buy tickets the day of the game because games weren't sold out back then. We sat in the bleachers in left field, right in front of where Alan Ameche scored the winning touchdown for the Colts in overtime. The hole was so big you could have driven several trucks through it.

"I was there for some times when the Giants stunk up the joint. By the end of a poor season, you'd see people get frustrated and start throwing snowballs from the stands. I never did, though there were times I was tempted to. The players wouldn't have had anything to worry about because my arm wasn't strong enough to reach them, anyway."

## DANNY AND DAVID MANTLE

Mickey Mantle's two surviving sons have many fond memories of accompanying their dad to his "office," which just happened to be Yankee Stadium. Danny and David reside in the Dallas area and help manage their father's estate.

Danny: "The clubhouse guys, Big Pete and Little Pete Sheehy would always take care of us whenever Dad took us to the stadium. They'd get us a hot dog and a bottle of Yoo-hoo chocolate milk and tons of baseball cards and bubble gum, and we'd be as happy as a pig in mud. I remember us having to get there early because Dad would have to soak his legs in the whirlpool, then tape them up like a mummy. We'd pretty much leave him alone, unless we had a question. We were allowed to go out to the dugout and onto the field as long as we didn't mess anything up. I remember throwing footballs around in the outfield, and when batting practice began we had to go to the dugout so we wouldn't get hurt. About 30 minutes before the game, we'd get booted upstairs, and we'd be sitting in the stands with the other players' kids. They usually were pretty good seats, often behind home plate. But we didn't care because we'd always be running around, terrorizing the other kids and the fans. For me, it was like being in this big playground.

"I knew when Dad was coming up because there would be a buzz in the stands. But we were young kids just having fun, so we didn't really pay much attention. To us, that was just Dad doing his job like any other dad at work. His work just happened to be baseball, and his office just happened to be Yankee Stadium. One game, he hit home runs batting righty and lefty. When we got back to our home in New Jersey, he joked that we probably didn't even know he had smacked two homers that day, and he was right.

David: "Dad wouldn't allow us to be bat boys because we had it pretty good already. He wanted other kids to have a chance at that. We'd spend some time before games in the locker room with our dad, and he let us stay there as long as we didn't bother any of the players. We just hung around with the other kids and the Sheehys. I remember all the old wires and the narrow hallways and corridors down in the bowels of the stadium. The locker rooms weren't very plush. They certainly didn't have any recliners in there the way guys do today.

"We couldn't help but notice how people in New York loved Dad. He couldn't go anywhere without being swarmed. He'd park his car in the players' lot, and we'd start walking toward the stadium, and he'd be surrounded by kids wanting his autograph. He always would sign, but he couldn't do it for long because he always needed a lot of treatment for his bad legs. I know he appreciated the way people felt about him, but we could see how demanding it could get. I think that's why he liked his time in the offseason back in Dallas. He could be a little more anonymous there. In New York he couldn't go anywhere without people creating a fuss over him.

"It's been so great for Danny and me to come back for several occasions when they've honored Dad. They had that ceremony about a year ago unveiling the postage stamp he's on, and one of the most special days was back in 1996 when they unveiled the monument to Dad. Danny, myself, and Mom got to say a few words and throw out the ceremonial first pitches. I remember being out there and looking up into the stands and feeling so good about the fact that so many people still loved Dad."


## BISHOP MATTHEW CLARK

Roughly three months after being ordained as bishop of the Diocese of Rochester, New York, Matthew Clark attended the mass celebrated by Pope John Paul II at Yankee Stadium on October 2, 1979. For Clark, the religious ceremony had extra meaning because he had grown up a Yankees fan in Waterford, New York, near Albany. He was one of nearly 80,000 on hand for the pontiff's first visit to the United States.

"The Yankees have been a great interest of mine for years. My favorite player growing up was Yogi Berra. I don't know what it was about him. I just like him. I found him a very attractive character. He always seemed to come through when you needed him, and he was very versatile. He could play the outfield as well as catch. I also liked some of the lesser-known, but still important Yankees, players such as Bobby Richardson and Gil McDougald.

"When I received word that the pope's mass would be held at the stadium, it brought a smile to my face and brought back fond memories of trips I had made there with my father when I was just a boy.

*Pope John Paul II celebrates mass at Yankee Stadium on October 2, 1979.*

"I was with a group of bishops who dressed in the Yankees clubhouse, which I had never been in before or since. The locker I used to hang my jacket and things had been used by a young pitcher named Dave Righetti. That was 1979, and both Dave Righetti and I were considerably younger than we are now. I guess you could say that we were both in the early stages of our careers—he as a promising pitcher for the Yankees, and me as a new bishop.

"Baseball stadiums have been called green cathedrals, and I remember how beautifully they had set up Yankee Stadium for this occasion. You didn't have the sense that you were in some vast place. The altar was set up in shallow center field in such a way that the three decks of the stadium bent around it, almost like arms reaching out around you. The park lent itself for lots of space for motion and procession. It looked very dignified and beautiful. I don't think there was a person there who didn't think the setting was appropriate for such a sacred occasion.

"My recollection is that Pope John Paul II was certainly cordial and warm, but also very challenging in his message to the citizenry of the Catholic Church in America. He used a gospel story to remind us that we've been profoundly blessed with material goods and that we need to share those riches with the equivalent of Lazarus, meaning the poor, the ostracized, the dispossessed, both in our country and throughout the world. It was a very powerful message, and one that certainly moved the tens of thousands who had come to hear it from a man who was beloved."

**OFF THE WALL**
**Spinning turnstiles: The Yankees set a franchise and American League attendance record in 2007 when they drew 4,271,083 fans to the stadium. The largest single-game crowd was 81,841 for a game against the Boston Red Sox on May 30, 1938.**

# ED SHAW

Shaw will be the first to tell you that it isn't easy being a Yankees fan near the epicenter of Red Sox Nation. And it's even harder when your father convinces your daughters to cheer for Boston.

"Although we lived in New York, first in Queens and then in Rye, my dad did his best to convince my brother Stu and me that Boston's professional sports teams were the ones to root for. My dad was a native of Quincy, Massachusetts, and it seemed like every year we were watching the Boston Celtics win another championship, although the Knicks did upset his apple cart twice while I was in high school in '70 and '73. When Bobby Orr and Espo were winning Stanley cups in '70 and '72, I had to endure derisive cackles about the Rangers 'overrated' GAG [goal-a-game] line. His Red Sox made their runs, of course, in '67, '75, '78, and '86, but we all know what happened there.

"I had been to the stadium a number of times, as a grade-schooler, to see the football Giants play with Dad, but the first and last Yankee game I went to with him was in celebration of his 70th birthday on May 24, 1997. It was Memorial Day weekend and the Red Sox were in town. My daughters, Amanda, age 10, and Catie, age 8, and I, along with my brother and his son, Ian, age 5, made the trek to the stadium with 'Grand Pa.' In addition to the family generational dynamic, there was also a Red Sox–versus–Yankees component at play. My girls were growing up in a Boston suburb and were vehemently aligned with my dad in their support of the Red Sox, while the rest of us were committed Yankees fans.

"Our seats were up in the third deck, just a little to the third-base side from home plate. It was a comfortably warm, only partially cloudy day with a bright sun. The U.S. Navy had an aircraft carrier and other large ships docked in the city, and there were sailors everywhere you looked as part of a Fleet Day promotion. As an ex-Navy man, my dad was enjoying himself to no end striking up conversations with all the young seamen who had just arrived in the Big Apple. In fact I had to track my dad down from the concourse to get him to come back to our seats in time to see the surprise birthday message I had arranged for months beforehand that appeared on the score-board in the middle of the fifth inning. We all got a big kick out of his look of surprise in seeing his name up in lights along with those of his grandkids wishing him happy birthday. It was rare to see Dad speechless.

"We swapped seats often, and everyone got to spend some quality time with Dad. The adults would come and go during the game, taking the kids to get something to eat or to accompany them to the bathroom. Stu and I shared a few beers with Dad and talked about all sorts of things at that game in between the action on the field. I remember Dad telling the girls that he was glad that they hadn't been 'corrupted by their father' the way Ian had been by his dad and become Yankees fans. This comment elicited giggles from the girls and hugs for their grandfather, to which I could only slowly shake my head back and forth in mock disbelief.

"The game itself was competitive, with the Yankees winning via a walk-off home run in the ninth inning. I reminded my dad that this was the way things were supposed to be. It was the 'natural order of things,' I told him. I would pay for that comment in 2004.

"When we got back to my parents' house, we had cake and ice cream. As a special gift for Dad, I had all three grandkids sign a Red Sox–logoed baseball. The ball had the date along with the final score on it as well, and we put it in a protective case for him. It was the end to a perfect day.

"Eight years later, the vibrant man who was my father would be stricken with terminal brain cancer. He died three months after he was diagnosed. Dad passed away at home surrounded by his family. Next to his bed was his dresser.

> **OFF THE WALL**
> A crowd of 123,707 worshippers attended a Jehovah's Witnesses convention at the stadium on August 2, 1950—the largest single-day attendance in the ballpark's history.

Within his sight, on that dresser, there were only three items. The first two were a picture of his mother and a picture of my mom, his wife of 55 years. The third item was that baseball we gave him when we had no thoughts of life without him. I was heartened to think we had given back to him in some way for the lifetime of memories he had given us."

## DAVID RAMSEY

Ramsey took a break from covering Syracuse University basketball and writing sports columns to write about the welcoming rally for South African freedom fighter Nelson Mandela at the stadium on June 21, 1990. It remains one of the most memorable assignments for Ramsey, who's now a sports columnist in Colorado Springs.

"The image never will leave me. Nelson Mandela was dancing the dance of liberation on a stage at Yankee Stadium, surrounded

*Nelson Mandela, a human-rights activist and former political prisoner in South Africa, celebrates his newfound freedom at an antiapartheid rally at Yankee Stadium on June 21, 1990.*

by hundreds of South African exiles. One of the century's great freedom fighters was, amazingly, free.

"A few years earlier, I had stood atop Table Mountain in Cape Town, South Africa, looking far below at the fields of fynbos flowers and the silver trees and the waves crashing along the beaches. It was gorgeous, but also an excruciating moment. I was gazing at Robben Island, where Mandela had resided for decades as a prisoner. I expected him to die there. Everyone expected him to die there.

**OFF THE WALL**
**Yankee Stadium cost $2.5 million to construct in 1922–1923 and $160 million to renovate in 1974–1975.**

"At his trial in 1962, Mandela had the gall to announce, 'I have cherished the ideal of a democratic and free society in which all persons live together in harmony.... If needs be, it is an ideal for which I am prepared to die.'

"In the officially, unapologetically racist realm of South Africa, those words were heresy. The apartheid government sentenced Mandela to life in the nation's vicious prison system.

"But international pressure finally forced the government to release Mandela, and on a June night in 1990, he was standing in front of me and 50,000 others at Yankee Stadium. He was fresh from prison, but life behind bars had done nothing to dull a natural showman. He placed the famous NY cap on his head and announced, 'I am a Yankee.'

"Yet it was more than a mere show. He spoke powerfully of human rights, of the evil of bigotry, and of the absolute requirement for forgiveness.

"I sat next to a South African woman who had fled her native country. Her husband had been an activist against apartheid, and one afternoon a band of the government police snatched him away and took him to a dank prison. Months later, the woman walked into her kitchen and saw an emaciated man. She had no idea who he was. He looked at her for several seconds. She stared back. He kept waiting for recognition. 'I am,' he said, 'your husband.' He had been starved and beaten beyond recognition.

"They soon escaped to the United States. Tears rolled down the cheeks of the South African woman as she joined Mandela in the dance steps of her homeland.

"Yet she was beaming, her face a joyful reminder that evil can sometimes be conquered. On this warm, happy summer night, we all joined Mandela in his unlikely victory."

## DELORES SOIFER

A first-grade teacher in Westchester County, the Bronx-born-and-raised Soifer has been attending games since the early 1950s.

"Back then they used to allow the fans to walk across the field after games, and I remember grabbing a bagful of dirt from the diamond. I still have it in one of my drawers in my house. It's my special keepsake.

"One of my biggest thrills was going to the stadium at 5:00 in the morning and waiting on line to buy bleacher seats for the World Series. It must have been '52 or '53. We wound up getting six bleacher seats, and I remember watching Mickey Mantle hit one of his World Series homers. That was quite a thrill.

"I grew up two train stops from the stadium, so I used to come to a lot of games. It was 10¢ for the subway, and you used to be able to bring soda and peanuts into the ballpark. Once, when I was 14 years old, I came here for a night game that went into extra, extra innings. They actually had to call it at midnight and resume it the next day because there was a curfew in the Bronx back then that said the lights had to go out at 12:00.

> **OFF THE WALL**
> **A Hammond organ was installed in the stadium in 1967, and Eddie Layton tickled the ivories from that season through the 2003 campaign.**

"I have mixed feelings about them building the new stadium. If you think about it, this place really changed quite a bit when they renovated it in the 1970s. It's like this became The House That Ruth Built No. 2, and the place across the street will be The House That Ruth Built No. 3. It's gonna be sad, but I guess time marches on."

## GORDON ARNOLD

A native of Saskatchewan, Canada, Arnold remembers listening to Subway Series games between the Yankees and Dodgers on the radio in the one-room school he attended near the Montana border. Sixteen years ago, at age 56, he visited the stadium for the first time and has been making pilgrimages there from Canada ever since.

"We'd listen to Yankees games all the time, and I remember being a big fan of right fielder Hank Bauer. He was a fiery guy. And years later, I became a fan of Paul O'Neill because he had that same kind of infectious competitiveness that Bauer had. Kept everybody on their toes.

"We started getting the Yankees games on television, so that was a treat. And I've seen them play the Twins in Minneapolis and the Blue Jays up in the Rogers Centre in Toronto. But there's nothing like Yankee Stadium. The first time I came here it took my breath away. It was like visiting a religious shrine, it really was. Now, I try to get back here whenever I can because this is my team and this is my place. You can't beat it for excitement."

## JOHN CUNIBERTI

He grew up in New Jersey and remembers attending his first Yankee game when he was 11 years old, and Joe DiMaggio was still roaming center field.

"I remember being here when Babe Ruth made his final public appearance [in 1948]. He was quite sick and emaciated, and his voice was hoarse and raspy because of the throat cancer. It was really sad to see him that way.

"I'm 76 now, and I can remember the sights and the sounds like I did when I was a kid. A ballpark like this can do that to you—take you back in time. It's always been kind of a magical place. You walk in from the streets in the Bronx and you come through the tunnel up to the stands and you see this huge green expanse, and it's kind of mind-boggling, really. It still has that effect on me all these years later."

## LOUIS COPPOLA

A former producer and engineer for CBS who worked with the likes of Dan Rather, Charles Osgood, and Charles Kuralt, Coppola has attended numerous games through the years. But one sticks out for the 71-year-old from Englewood, New Jersey—the day in 1993 when Jim Abbott pitched a no-hitter for the Yankees against Cleveland.

"To this day, I don't know how he did it—not just the no-hitter, but being able to play major league baseball with just one hand. As I watched him get those final outs in the ninth inning to wrap it up, I thought about what this young man had to overcome to get to this moment. It brought tears to my eyes, and, believe me, I wasn't alone. There were a lot of people in the stands that day crying. It was so inspirational. It really made you think about how foolish it is, the trivial things we worry about, when you see what obstacles this guy has overcome."

## MATT MICHAEL

Michael grew up in Allentown, Pennsylvania, went to Penn State, and covered minor league baseball for the *Syracuse Post-Standard* for more than a decade.

"As a Yankees fan since the early 1970s—Horace Clarke, anyone?—I have been privileged to witness many historic events at the stadium. I was there on Old-Timers' Day in 1978, when Bob Sheppard announced that Billy Martin would return as the Yankees' manager in 1979. I was there on August 7, 1983, when the Yankees had a day for my all-time favorite player, Bobby Murcer. And I was there for some of the most memorable home runs in postseason history (Tino Martinez, Derek Jeter, and Scott Brosius in 2001, and Aaron Boone in 2003).

"But the Yankee Stadium moment I'll most remember occurred in a game the Yankees were losing at the time. After eight innings of Game 5 of the 2001 World Series, the Yanks trailed the Arizona Diamondbacks 2–0. New York was in danger of falling behind three games to two with Randy Johnson and Curt Schilling—the new millennium's Koufax and Drysdale—scheduled to pitch the next two games for the D-backs in Arizona.

"I spent Game 5 sitting in the Yankees' audio booth (right next to Sheppard's booth) with Chris Granozio, a friend who was the Yanks' music man at the time. As the Yankees took the field in the top of the ninth, we heard the fans starting to chant. We couldn't make it out, partly because the sound was muffled in the booth.

"Within seconds, though, the chant became loud and clear. Knowing Paul O'Neill was going to retire and this was his last inning at the stadium, the 56,000 fans were chanting "PAUL O'NEILL!" to the same rhythm as "LET'S GO YANKEES!"

"The moment sent chills down my spine, for many reasons. O'Neill was my favorite Yankee at the time, cut out of the same mold as one of my other childhood heroes, Thurman Munson. The fact that the fans responded that way when the Yankees were losing a World Series game made it even more special in my eyes.

"That game on November 1 was played only seven weeks after the terrorist attacks, and I've always believed that 9/11 had a lot to do with the fans' spontaneous salute to O'Neill. Like a cop or fireman, O'Neill was cheered for the all-out effort he gave the Yankees, and winning or losing a baseball game really didn't matter in the big picture.

"The Yankees, of course, came back to win that game. Brosius tied it in the bottom of the ninth with a two-out home run off Byung-Hyun Kim, and Alfonso Soriano's single won it in the twelfth. Still, I'll always remember that game as the Paul O'Neill game."

## DAN GUILFOYLE

A longtime sales executive for radio stations in upstate New York, Guilfoyle was raised in the New York City area and attended Fordham University in the Bronx. He grew up a New York Giants fan and expended much energy arguing with his neighborhood friends that Willie Mays was a better center fielder than Mickey Mantle and Duke Snider.

"The thing I remember about Yankee Stadium was the size. Even though I had been to the Polo Grounds and it had so much acreage, it seemed smaller than the stadium. Went to my first game there in 1954. My friend was a Chicago White Sox fan who liked Nellie Fox, so we went to see the ChiSox versus the Yanks. Although I was a Mays fan, I remember being kind of in awe of Mickey Mantle. I couldn't believe how hard he swung. But he only got a few hits in the times I saw him, and that made me and one of my friends who was a Snider fan quite happy. We would get caught up in the Willie, Mickey, and the Duke arguments, and that was really stupid because you weren't going to convince anybody that you were right. We all liked our guys, and that was that.

"Back in 1974, I was living in Rochester, and I told a friend I was going to be in New York, and he invited me to a Yankees game. When he said he had season tickets behind home plate, I said, 'I'm in.' We go out to dinner before the game and I'm excited about these seats, so I buy. We get to the stadium and we start going up. And up. And up. We finally stopped climbing about three rows from the roof. He wasn't lying. The seats were indeed behind home plate. I just didn't know I'd need high-powered binoculars to see the game."

**OFF THE WALL**

After the first pitch of the game is delivered, the Bleacher Creatures in section 39 begin their roll call of Yankees players. They start by chanting the name of the Yankees center fielder, and after he acknowledges their chant, they move on to the right fielder and go right on down the line. When the rival Boston Red Sox are in town, the Creatures occasionally will chant the names of Red Sox tormentors, such as Babe Ruth, Bucky Dent, and Aaron Boone.

# MEMBERS OF MEDIA
# REMINISCE

## BOB COSTAS

A broadcaster with NBC since the early 1980s, Costas has won nearly 20 Emmy Awards and has been named national sportscaster of the year more than 10 times. He has been his network's anchor for coverage of the NFL and several Olympics, but the Queens native's number one sporting passion always has been baseball. He began following the Yankees in the 1950s, and like millions of American boys of that era, he imitated the batting, running, and fielding mannerisms of Yankees center fielder Mickey Mantle. For many years, Costas carried a 1958 Mantle baseball card in his wallet, and he later became friends with the Yankees legend. When Mantle died of liver cancer in 1995, the family asked Costas to deliver the eulogy, and he did so with eloquence and just the right touch of humor. Costas has many special memories of Yankee Stadium. He still remembers walking onto the field following a game and wondering if Babe Ruth and Lou Gehrig were actually buried under their monuments.

"One of the things that always struck me about the place was how extreme the dimensions were and what an effect they had on the game. It was very short down both lines, and very short to straightaway right, with a low fence, which made for some short, pop-fly homers as well as some acrobatic catches. I can still visualize right fielders like Roger Maris and Al Kaline and Frank Robinson making catches where they tumbled into the stands and wound up two or three rows deep.

**OFF THE WALL**

**The 138-foot-tall Louisville Slugger outside the stadium's main entrance is actually a boiler stack. Designed to look like a bat Babe Ruth used, the tower is used by many spectators as a meeting place before games.**

"A ball hit sharply down the lines was very likely to either bounce in for a ground-rule double or come around the curve of the wall and pose a problem for the pursuing left fielder or right fielder.

"At the same time, it was 402 feet to straight-away left and then you got out to 457 feet in the left-center power alley and 461 feet to dead center with a fence so high, they had a list in the Yankees yearbook of every ball that had been hit over that wall. And there was only something like 15 homers listed, and Mantle had about six of them. Any ball that got hit out there had to be a real bomb. And don't forget, this was the era before steroids and with an elevated pitching mound, so those were titanic shots.

"The other thing about those deep fences is that, if you did poke one over the center fielder's head, you immediately thought there was the possibility of an inside-the-park home run—something you don't usually see today unless two outfielders happen to collide.

"If possible, you wanted to pitch left-handers at the stadium so you could prevent left-handed batters from taking advantage of that short porch in right. That's what the Dodgers did in the 1963 World Series. Walter Alston started with Sandy Koufax and came back with another lefty, Johnny Podres, because the first two games were at Yankee Stadium. He actually saved his second-best pitcher, Don Drysdale, for Game 3 back in L.A. The strategy worked to perfection as the Dodgers swept the Series.

"I remember, as a teenager, going to a midweek game in August of 1964. It was one of those times when you go to a game thinking it's going to be like any other game and something historical happens. The Yankees were hooked up in a tight pennant race at the time and were trailing the White Sox and Orioles. They had just brought up Mel Stottlemyre from Richmond, and it was Stottlemyre's big-league debut. It also turned out to be the last time Mantle homered lefty and righty in the same game. And the first of those two homers was a shot over the dead-center-field fence off of Ray Herbert. I remember when Mantle hit the ball, he sort of flipped his bat in disgust as he sometimes did, and the ball kept on going and going and going. The center fielder for the White Sox was Gene Stephens, whose claim to fame was getting three hits in one inning for the Boston Red Sox.

"The day after Mantle's homers, there was a full-page picture on the back page of the [New York] *Daily News* of Stephens with his back to home plate. The ball was hit so high that Stephens actually got all the way back to the wall, thinking he could catch it. The ball wound up landing in the seats, and there was one guy sitting out there, and he didn't get up to get the ball, so that allowed someone from the Yankees PR department to get the ball. They estimate that the ball went 503 feet.

> **OFF THE WALL**
> In 1966–1967, the stadium's brown concrete exterior and copper green façade were painted white, and all of the green grandstand seats were painted blue.

"Then, later in the same game, batting right-handed, Mantle homered off Don Mossi into the upper deck in right field, marking the 10th and last time Mickey did the righty-lefty thing in a game.

"It also was Stottlemyre's first big-league win, and I think he wound up going 9–3 down the stretch as the Yankees came back to win the pennant. It's funny, but I can remember every last detail of this, and it's 43 years ago, but I couldn't give you that kind of detail about a Cardinals-Nationals game I saw yesterday. I was 12 years old, and I guess I cared about it more and was less distracted. It had my complete, undivided attention."

# ERNIE HARWELL

Former Brooklyn Dodgers general manager Branch Rickey was so enamored with Harwell's folksy broadcasting style that he actually traded one of his minor league players in order to acquire Harwell from the old Atlanta Crackers. Thus began a career in the radio and television booth that would span 55 years, including 42 seasons with the Detroit Tigers. Along the way, Harwell would work numerous regular- and postseason games for the networks. In 1981, he became the fifth baseball announcer to receive the prestigious Ford C. Frick Award from the National Baseball Hall of Fame.

"I actually called football games before I worked baseball games at Yankee Stadium. The Dodgers had a team in the old All-American Football Conference in the 1940s, and Mr. Rickey asked me if I wouldn't mind broadcasting their games, too. Let's just say, it wasn't the greatest assignment I've ever had in my career. The Dodgers didn't win a game the season I did their games, and, to be honest, Yankee Stadium wasn't the best place to broadcast a football game. But I was young and full of vim and vigor, so I survived.

"I obviously go way back with Yankee Stadium. I really think the ballpark lost a little bit of its character when they renovated it in the early 1970s. But it still was a historic place after the renovations. There's still an aura about it. Every time I'm there, I'm thinking that Ruth and Gehrig once played here, and that's hard to top.

**OFF THE WALL**
After 9/11, all major league ballparks started playing "God Bless America" during the seventh-inning stretch. Other teams stopped playing the song the following season, but the Yankees have continued the tradition ever since. A taped rendition by the late Kate Smith usually is played, but occasionally Irish tenor Ronan Tynan will perform the song live.

"I broadcast a lot of games there when I was with the Orioles and then the Tigers. Plus, I did a bunch of playoff games there for various networks. I remember being there when Hall of Fame third baseman George Brett hit three home runs for the Kansas City Royals against the Yankees. That was special—unless, of course, you were a Yankees fan.

"One of the most interesting games I did there occurred in the mid-1950s. I was broadcasting for Baltimore and I saw Mickey Mantle hit a single that bounced into the center-field bleachers to win a ballgame. It should have been a double, but wasn't because of the situation. The Yankees and Baltimore were tied in extra innings and the bases were loaded when Mickey hit this shot to center field. Ordinarily, it would have been a double, but the scoring rules only allowed a single because the bases were stacked. That was back in the days when it was more than 450 feet to the bleachers, and the wall was pretty high, so that was quite a wallop. Anyplace else it would have been a grand slam. I like to tell people that I broadcast the longest single in baseball history that day."

## PHIL PEPE

Pepe grew up in Brooklyn, rooting for the Dodgers and hating the Yankees. But when he became a baseball writer for the old *New York World-Telegram & Sun* in 1961, he had to put aside his youthful disdain for the Bronx Bombers. During the next three decades, mostly with the *[New York] Daily News,* Pepe would cover the Yankees and be on hand for some of the greatest moments in stadium history—Roger Maris's 61st homer, Mickey Mantle's blast that ricocheted off the façade, Chris Chambliss's walk-off homer in the 1976 playoffs, and Reggie Jackson's three-home-run performance in the 1977 World Series. Pepe would go on to write nearly 50 books, including the authorized history of the Yankees and a recounting of Mantle's Triple Crown season in 1956. These days, he continues to write books as well as a column for the YES Network website.

"In 1951 one of my uncles procured tickets to Game 1 of the World Series at Yankee Stadium, and I was all revved up because I figured it was going to be the Yankees versus my beloved Dodgers. Well, lo and behold, Bobby Thomson wound up hitting his famous home run in that playoff game, and it turned out that the Giants, not the Dodgers, were going to be playing. I

*Roger Maris's phenomenal swing allowed him to hit 61 home runs in 1961 to break Babe Ruth's record.*

swallowed my pride and went anyway, and I decided I'd root for the Giants to win because I figured if they beat the Yankees that would mean Brooklyn was the second best team in baseball. I remember that game vividly because Monte Irvin stole home and the Giants won Game 1. So I left the stadium that day feeling a little vindicated. Never mind that the Yankees wound up winning the Series.

"I remember being overwhelmed by the sheer size of the place. I had gone to games at Ebbets Field and the Polo Grounds, and they were bandboxes compared to the stadium.

"A decade later, after I graduated from St. John's, I was back at the stadium in a working capacity. I was there for Maris's 61st home run, which was interesting in retrospect because there were only about 23,000 fans there that day. Today, if you had somebody going for such a historic mark, the place would be sold out. I had taken over the Yankees beat during the second half of that season, and my editors told me that, no matter what, I was to write about Mantle and Maris every day because that's who everybody was interested in. It was a very exciting time, watching them make their assault on Ruth's single-season home-run record, and I can remember the toll it took on Roger. I was there when clumps of his hair began falling out because of all the stress he was under. Roger just wanted to play ball; he didn't care for the attention. He could be difficult at times, but I don't recall him being a jerk.

"That, of course, was the year when the fans' perception of Mickey Mantle really started to change. For the longest time, the fans at the stadium had booed Mantle because he hadn't—in their minds—lived up to the enormous hype, and he struck out too much. But in 1961 Mickey became the people's choice. If Ruth's record was going to fall, the majority of the fans wanted to see a Yankees legend like Mickey do it. In his movie, *61\**, Billy Crystal portrayed the sportswriters as rooting against

Maris. That wasn't really true. Sure, baseball purists like me wanted to see Mantle break it, but we weren't against Maris. In fact I wanted to see one of them do it because I realized the historical significance of it, and I wanted to be there for baseball history.

"After Roger finally did it on the last day of the season, I remember his teammates having to push him out of the dugout so he could take a curtain call. Today guys hop out of the dugout for the most insignificant things.

"I remember a young man named Sal Durante caught the home-run ball, and when they brought him in to meet Roger after the game, he wanted to give Roger the ball in exchange for a baseball autographed by Maris. Roger had heard that Sal was planning to get married, so he told Sal to keep the ball and sell it so he could pay for the wedding. He wound up getting something like $10,000 for the ball, which is pocket change compared to what it would go for had that happened today. I thought that was a really nice gesture on Roger's part.

"I was there in '63 when Mantle missed by inches hitting the first fair ball out of the stadium. He hit it off Bill Fischer of the Kansas

City Athletics, and it smashed against the façade hanging from the roof in right field. It got up there so quickly, you were stunned by the enormity of it. It occurred a day or two after Astronaut [Gordon] Cooper had orbited the earth, and I remember writing that Mantle's ball should be arriving up there any time now.

"I guess those two homers, plus Reggie's three-homer Series game and the 18-strikeout performance by Ron Guidry against the California Angels are the four most memorable games I covered there.

"I also covered a fight there in 1959 in which Ingemar Johansson fought Floyd Patterson. I remember Joe DiMaggio showing up and walking down the aisle from home plate to third base, and as he passed people, they got up and gave him a standing ovation. From my vantage point ringside, it looked almost like the fans were doing the wave. Joe's entrance as a spectator was more memorable to me than the fight itself.

"I had the opportunity to pitch several times at Yankee Stadium. They would stage games between the writers and Yankee office personnel, and sometimes a former Yankee like Gene Michael or Charley Lau would join in. Charley Lau actually lined one of my pitches into the right-field seats for a home run. Being out there on the mound gave me an entirely different perspective than I got from covering games from the press box. When you are on that mound, you really appreciate just how cavernous the stadium is. You begin to understand why pitchers battle nerves standing out there, looking at 55,000 people.

"My first child was actually born while I was covering a game at the stadium in 1962. I brought my wife to the hospital, and back in those days the fathers weren't allowed in the birthing room. In fact, that day, the nurse told me not to wait around. She said, 'Go to work, and we'll give you a call.' So I headed to the stadium, and about the fourth inning I got the call in the press box telling me that my daughter, Jayne, was born. There was a roar in the crowd as she was telling me, and she asked me where I was, and I said, 'Yankee Stadium.' She didn't know I was a sportswriter, so she must have thought I was pretty insensitive. But I was just following instructions. She said to go to work, and I had. Word spread quickly through the press box, and before I left for the hospital, Bob Sheppard, handed me a poem he had written about my daughter. Bob was always writing poems and limericks. I think my daughter still has it."

## DICK VITALE

He's become college's basketball's most recognizable voice, but long before he became a ubiquitous hoops guru for ESPN, Vitale followed the Yankees with the same fervor he now shows during basketball telecasts. The New Jersey native made plenty of trips across the bridges in the 1950s and '60s to watch his heroes play.

"As a teenager, I remember going with a buddy of mine to Yankee Stadium during a day when the Yankees were on the road to buy tickets for an upcoming game. One of the gates was open, so we were able to sneak into the stadium and get onto the field. We couldn't believe our good fortune. We ran around the bases. We went to the mound and pretended we were Whitey Ford and threw imaginary pitches. We sat in the Yankees dugout and made believe we were stars being interviewed by reporters after hitting game-winning homers.

**OFF THE WALL**
**Prodding by Hollywood legend Cary Grant reportedly convinced owner George Steinbrenner to keep the trademark frieze (façade) when the stadium was renovated.**

"We were like the proverbial kids in the candy shop. We had the whole place to ourselves. Yankee Stadium was our playground—until this angry maintenance guy spotted us and threw us out. It was one of the great thrills of my young life to be on the same grounds where the Babe and Joe D once tread. I had goose bumps all the way back to Jersey. You talk about awesome, baby. I was so hyped up, I couldn't sleep that night.

"We used to try to get there on game days in time for batting practice, because that was your best chance of getting a ball. And when we did, we'd trade them to some young, rich kid in exchange for their tickets to their box seats.

"The first time, though, that I got a ball, I wasn't going to trade it for anything. I was out in the left-field seats during batting practice and I kept begging the old relief pitcher, Joe Page, for a ball. He finally relented and tossed one to me. I was so nervous I dropped it, and a bunch of kids came running over, but they didn't have a chance. I fell on that ball and smothered it like it was the Hope Diamond.

"In recent years I've had the opportunity to sit in the VIP box next to the dugout—the seats where Rudy Giuliani and Billy Crystal usually sit, and each time I'm there, I'm like that little kid I used to be all over again. I'm 68 but I feel 10 when I'm sitting there. It reminds me of the first time my uncles took me there and the Yankees were playing the Cleveland Indians and I saw the great DiMaggio. Years later, I became a big Willie Mays fan and I had friends who were big Mickey Mantle fans and big Duke Snider fans, so we would get into arguments. And my dad and my uncles would hear us and say that Joe D. never had to dive for a ball because he always got a great jump on the ball. They'd say, 'Boys, end of discussion.'"

## BOB WOLFF

He began his broadcasting career while a student at Duke University back in 1939, and at age 86 he continues to work on both television and radio in the New York City area—making him the longest-running act in broadcasting. A New York native who remembers going to games at the stadium when Babe Ruth played, Wolff has done it all and seen it all. He is one of the few broadcasters to have called a World Series, the NBA Finals, the Stanley Cup Finals, and an NFL championship game. He received the Ford Frick Award from the National Baseball Hall of Fame in 1995. Of all the games he has covered, he's best known for calling the final innings of Don Larsen's perfect game in the 1956 World Series on the national radio broadcast.

"The way it was set up back then, there were no such things as color men. There were no athletes in the booth, just announcers. At the Series, one guy would do the pregame show and the final four innings of the game, while the other announcer would do the first five innings, and you would rotate the next game. In Larsen's perfect game, I had the good fortune to do the second half of the game.

"At the halfway point, I spoke to the producer, Joel Nixon, about how we should handle the final four innings because Larsen was working on the no-hitter, and back then you still had this strong superstition about not using the word *no-hitter* on broadcasts. I told Joel that I wanted everybody around the country to know at all times that there was a no-hitter in progress, but I didn't want to use those exact words until the end, when we reached the climax.

"In the 1947 World Series, Floyd ["Bill"] Bevens was working on a no-hitter for the Yankees, and the famous announcer Red Barber used the word *no-hitter* several times in those final innings. Well, the Brooklyn Dodgers wound up breaking up the no-hitter and winning the game when Cookie Lavagetto

*New York Yankees catcher Yogi Berra leaps into the arms of pitcher Don Larsen after Larsen struck out the last Brooklyn Dodgers batter to complete his perfect game during Game 5 of the 1956 World Series on October 8, 1956.* Photo courtesy of AP/Wide World Images.

lined a ball off the right-field wall to drive in the tying and winning runs.

"People were aghast that Red dare break tradition that way. Of course, Barber was one of the all-time greats. He said afterward, 'I'm just an honest reporter. You say what you see, what you know.' It seems kind of silly, because today, you've got everything flashed up there on the television screen. But back in the 1950s, baseball fans were really sensitive about that stuff, and sponsors would react to it if they were deluged with letters.

"I figured I could be an honest reporter without using the word *no-hitter*. I wound up using every synonym in the book— 'Eighteen up, 18 down. The only hit so far has been by the Yankees. No Dodger has reached base.' I was still able to keep people informed. That enabled me to save my climactic lines 'til the end. After Larsen got pinch-hitter Dale Mitchell on a called third strike to end the game, I said, 'It's a no-hitter, a perfect game for Don Larsen. Yogi Berra runs out, leaps into Larsen's arms. The crowd is roaring....' I was able to report the game accurately and still save my punch lines 'til the end.

"I was pleased with the volume of mail that came in about how much they liked the broadcast. Gillette, which held the sponsorship rights to the Series in those days, said, 'Okay, Bob, you're on the team.' And I wound up doing the Series again in 1958 and '61. NBC then hired me to do the *Game of the Week* and the Rose Bowl and Sugar Bowl, so the way I handled the broadcast of the perfect game wound up being a big moment in my life."

# KEITH OLBERMANN

A native New Yorker and Cornell University graduate, Olbermann hosts the highly rated *Countdown with Keith Olbermann* news show on MSNBC. The former ESPN *SportsCenter* anchor also is cohost of NBC's *Football Night in America* with Bob Costas. Olbermann is an avid baseball card collector and a longtime member of the Society for American Baseball Research (SABR).

"In 1967 Mickey Mantle was winding up his career with the Yankees at first base in order to try to save his knees, and my parents made this marvelous decision to purchase box seats behind first base that summer. They told me this will probably be one of your greatest thrills, if not your greatest thrill, watching Mickey Mantle play up close and personal, and they were right. I must have seen him play 20–25 times. I saw a game in 1968 in which he hit a homer, and this kid from the Oakland A's, in his second season, by the name of Reggie Jackson, also homered. That was pretty neat, watching two players who would wind up with 1,100 homers between them, spanning two pretty good generations of baseball. I guess I flash back mostly to Mantle when I think of Yankee Stadium.

"My most embarrassing moment occurred a year or two after Mickey retired. When I was 13, the people in the front box took the Fourth of July off, and they said, 'Use our seats while we are not here.' I was sitting in the front row, along the railing, and I completely forgot how close I was to the action. Fritz Peterson was pitching for the Yankees against the Boston Red Sox, and there was this foul pop from Rico Petrocelli that was heading toward us. It was extremely high and I decided to try to catch it. I'm reaching up to the sky and somehow I got turned around with my back actually to the field. I'm so focused on the ball that I don't realize I'm probably going to be greeted by a first baseman at some point. The ball nails me right in the hands and bounds about 20 feet back into the stands. My hand starts throbbing. I turn around, and glaring at me with his hands on his hips was the figure of Yankees first baseman Felipe Alou.

"The next pitch from Peterson to Petrocelli is a line-drive base hit up the middle. It was the first hit he gave up and, as

**OFF THE WALL**
**Beginning in 1971, the stadium hosted the Whitney M. Young Jr. Football Classic, which featured schools from "historically black colleges." The game, sponsored by the New York Urban League, often included Grambling State University of Louisiana, coached by Hall of Famer Eddie Robinson. Grambling wound up losing to Central State University of Ohio, 37–21, in 1987 in the last football game played at the stadium.**

it turned out, the only hit he gave up through seven or eight innings. By this point, I'm dying. Not only is my hand killing me, I'm thinking about how I've cost Fritz Peterson a no-hitter. Plus, I've been glared at by one of the players on my team.

"So years later, I'm watching the Chicago Cubs and the Florida Marlins in the 2003 playoffs and Felipe's son, Moises Alou, encounters a fan going after the ball in a little different circumstance. And I flash back to my own foolish decision. I know what this guy is feeling like because I've been there. Neither one of us wanted to screw things up for our respective teams. But when a baseball is in the air, irrational things can happen."

## HANK GREENWALD

An upstate New York native and a graduate of Syracuse University, Greenwald spent 20 years broadcasting Major League Baseball games, mostly for the San Francisco Giants. In between stints with the Giants, Greenwald broadcast Yankees games in 1987 and '88. His quick wit and clever plays on words made him one of the most entertaining baseball broadcasters of his generation.

"The first time I went to a game at Yankee Stadium was in 1947. Bobo Newsom was pitching for the Yankees, and he was somewhat of a character. They were playing the Philadelphia A's, and Newsom hit a ball back to the mound. Instead of running to first base, he headed for the dugout. The pitcher, who I think was a guy named Bill McCahan, held onto the ball; he wouldn't throw to first. Bobo moved slowly down to the end of the dugout closest to first base and all of a sudden made this mad dash from the dugout to first. McCahan's delayed throw still beat him. Of course, the minute Newsom walked away from the plate, he was out. But the two pitchers wound up putting on quite a show, nonetheless.

"I was working for a radio station out of Syracuse and worked out a deal where I was able to cover the World Series game at the stadium in 1963 where Sandy Koufax set the record by striking out 15 batters.

"The two years I broadcast Yankee games were lean seasons. But I did get a chance to watch Don Mattingly play every day, and that was something to see. In 1987 he went on that hitting spree where he tied the major league record by homering in eight consecutive games. Then the next year he broke the record for most grand slams in a season. The funny thing about that is that he hit one in spring training that year, and after the game he told me that was the first grand slam he had hit at any level—Little League, Pony League, high school, and the minors. I guess you could say he made up for lost time that summer when he hit six.

> **OFF THE WALL**
> The American bald eagle Challenger flies from the center-field bleachers to the pitcher's mound during selected "big" games.

"Another moment that sticks out is one of the Opening Days I covered at the stadium, when Minnesota pulled off a triple play against the Yankees. It happened so matter-of-factly that you had to remind yourself how significant the play was."

## CURT SMITH

The author of 12 books and a former speechwriter for the first President Bush, Smith is regarded as the foremost expert on baseball broadcasting. Several of his books deal with that subject, including his definitive *Voices of the Game*. His most recent book was a biography of former Yankees broadcasting legend Mel Allen. The University of Rochester professor currently is working on a book about Dodgers broadcaster Vin Scully.

> **OFF THE WALL**
> The 1930 and '31 Army-Navy football games were played at the stadium, with the Cadets winning the contests by scores of 6–0 and 17–7.

"I grew up in the tiny burg of Caledonia, New York—population 2,000—in the 1950s and '60s, and my introduction to Yankee Stadium was through Mel Allen's vivid radio descriptions and NBC television's *Game of the Week*. To me, it was this magical place—a combination of the Louvre, the Hermitage, and the Czar's Winter Palace. It was cavernous and dark and shadowy and completely magnificent. It had everything you wanted in a ballpark and more—the triple tiers, the grand façade, the dimensions that would befit the Roman Colosseum. It had a marvelous diversity of size and dimension. You could hit a 297-foot home run, which I think probably even Andy Carey did, and you could hit a 458-foot out, as many ballplayers did. You hit inside-the-park homers to the left- and right-center-field alleys, or you could go 0-for-4 and hit the ball a cumulative 1,700 feet, as I believe Harmon Killebrew once did.

"I should probably be deported for revealing this, but I didn't make it to Yankee Stadium until 2002. I was entranced by the place. The fans certainly contribute to its mystique. There is a buzz in that ballpark. I was struck by the fans' extraordinary knowledge and interest in the game there."

## GEORGE VECSEY

Vecsey is a longtime sports columnist for *The New York Times* as well as a bestselling author. A native New Yorker, he grew up rooting for the Brooklyn Dodgers and freely admits that he hated the Yankees as a kid and only grudgingly has come to admire them as an adult. Journalism runs in his family. Both his parents worked for newspapers, as did his brother, Peter, and his daughter, Laura, who went on to become a sports columnist for newspapers in Baltimore and Seattle.

"I grew up a New Yorker, but I was a Brooklyn Dodgers fan, so I suffered terribly at the hands of the Yankees as a kid, meaning that Yankee Stadium wasn't this reverential place to me, but rather a house of horrors. Anybody who knows me realizes I still carry that edge and those scars. I can't always keep that inner child suppressed. Yankee Stadium has always been that place where the 'other' team played, and sometimes I still feel that way all these years later.

"I've certainly seen great things there, both as a fan and a journalist. I was there when Babe Ruth said 'good-bye' in a hoarse voice ravaged by cancer while wearing a camel-hair coat on a warm summer day. I remember Ty Cobb coming up to bat in an Old-Timers' Game, and before the pitch was thrown, he pushed the catcher down and laid down a bunt. And I'm thinking to myself that, even as an old man, Cobb hadn't changed. He was still competitive and nasty.

"I remember one time, not as a reporter but as a friend, I caught Jim Bouton at the stadium on a day when the Yankees were off. Actually, it was during Martin Luther King's funeral, and baseball had called off all of its games. Jim needed to work out, so there in empty Yankee Stadium, Jim took the mound, and I squatted behind home plate in the same spot where Yogi and Bill Dickey and Elston Howard had positioned themselves so many times. Then I got to use the clubhouse and the sauna where Mickey and Whitey used to hang out. I caught as a sandlot kid, so that was quite a thrill to be able to do that in The House That Ruth Built.

"In 1956, when I was a freshman in college, my father got me an extra press pass for the World Series, and I was able to go into the clubhouses of both the Yankees and Dodgers and do some interviews. It just so happened that the next day I was back at Hofstra listening on the radio as Don Larsen threw his no-hitter. I guess you could say my timing was off. I went one day too soon.

*President George W. Bush throws the ceremonial first pitch before Game 3 of the 2001 World Series at Yankee Stadium on October 30, 2001.*

"I've covered a lot of big moments there. One of the most moving was Game 3 of the 2001 World Series. It was the first Series game in New York after 9/11, and George Bush came to town to throw out the first pitch. I'm definitely not a fan of the guy, but I was impressed that he would do that. He was a baseball guy, and he was saying that life goes on. The fans were chanting, 'U.S.A.!' after he delivered the ball. I think it was one of the few shining moments of his presidency, and one of the more emotional events I've witnessed at the stadium."

# Sources

## Books

Appel, Marty. *Now Pitching for the Yankees: Spinning the News for Mickey, Billy, and George.* Toronto: SportClassic Books, 2001.

Bondy, Filip. *Bleeding Pinstripes: A Season with the Bleacher Creatures at Yankee Stadium.* Champaign, Illinois: Sports Publishing, LLC, 2005.

Buscema, Dave. *Game of My Life: 20 Stories of Yankees Baseball.* Champaign, Illinois: Sports Publishing LLC, 2004.

Crystal, Billy. *700 Sundays.* New York: Warner Books, 2005.

Durso, Joe. *Yankee Stadium: Fifty Years of Drama.* Boston: Houghton Mifflin Company, 1972.

Herskowitz, Mickey, Danny Mantle, and David Mantle. *Mickey Mantle: Stories and Memorabilia from a Lifetime with the Mick.* New York: Stewart, Tabori, and Chang, 2007.

Howe, Randy, ed. *The Yankees Fanatic.* Guilford, Connecticut: The Lyons Press, 2007.

Mantle, Mickey, and Herb Gluck. *The Mick.* New York: Doubleday, 1985.

Mantle, Mickey, and Phil Pepe. *My Favorite Summer: 1956.* New York: Doubleday, 1991.

Pepe, Phil. *The Yankees: An Authorized History of the New York Yankees.* Boulder, Colorado: Taylor Trade Publishing, 2003.

Robinson, Ray, and Christopher Jennison. *Yankee Stadium: 75 Years of Drama, Glamor, and Glory.* New York: Penguin Studio, 1998.

Tan, Cecilia. *The 50 Greatest Yankee Games.* Hoboken, New Jersey: John Wiley and Sons, 2005.


## OTHER SOURCES

Yankees.com
*Rochester (N.Y.) Democrat and Chronicle*
*The New York Times*
[New York] *Daily News*
*New York Post*
*Newsday*
*Sports Illustrated*
*Oprah* magazine
New York Yankees Yearbooks (1965–2007)
New York Yankees Media Guide (2007)